Praise for **The Leader's Guide to Emotional Agility**

'An excellent addition to *The Leader's Guide* series. A valuable resource full of strategies, tactics and insights about emotional acuity to help improve your knowledge, understanding and skill.'

Fiona Elsa Dent, management trainer, leadership coach and author

'This book will guide you to harness values and emotions to create favourable outcomes during transactions with team members and others in the work place.'

Aruna Anand, Director, Continental Engineering Services N.A.

'Managing people requires emotional agility, and Kerrie Fleming provides hands-on, practical strategies on how managers can effectively manage their own and other's emotions. Whether you are looking to prevent your own burn-out or for ways to inspire your team, you will find a clear path to doing so in her book.'

David R. Caruso Ph.D., co-founder, Emotional Intelligence Skills Group

'Practical, insightful and engaging, this book is a wonderful toolkit to support the development of a critical skill for today's leader.'

Tony Sheehan, Associate Dean, Digital Learning, London Business School

'Powerful and insightful, these seven small steps will help the reader make the huge leap from just leading to being a true leader. An essential read for leaders and those aspiring to climb up the corporate ladder.'

Professor Vicky Vass, Pro Vice-Chancellor, Buckinghamshire New University

'This book is a must read for leaders who believe that emotion unleashes action. For those who are sure they can reason their way to a good outcome, read something else.'

Richard Hytner, Deputy Chairman, Saatchi & Saatchi Worldwide

The Leader's Guide to
Emotional Agility

PEARSON

At Pearson, we believe in learning – all kinds of learning for all kinds of people. Whether it's at home, in the classroom or in the workplace, learning is the key to improving our life chances.

That's why we're working with leading authors to bring you the latest thinking and best practices, so you can get better at the things that are important to you. You can learn on the page or on the move, and with content that's always crafted to help you understand quickly and apply what you've learned.

If you want to upgrade your personal skills or accelerate your career, become a more effective leader or more powerful communicator, discover new opportunities or simply find more inspiration, we can help you make progress in your work and life.

Pearson is the world's leading learning company. Our portfolio includes the Financial Times and our education business, Pearson International.

Every day our work helps learning flourish, and wherever learning flourishes, so do people.

To learn more, please visit us at **www.pearson.com/uk**

The Financial Times

With a worldwide network of highly respected journalists, *The Financial Times* provides global business news, insightful opinion and expert analysis of business, finance and politics. With over 500 journalists reporting from 50 countries worldwide, our in-depth coverage of international news is objectively reported and analysed from an independent, global perspective.

To find out more, visit **www.ft.com/pearsonoffer/**

The Leader's Guide to Emotional Agility

How to use soft skills to get hard results

Kerrie Fleming

PEARSON

Harlow, England • London • New York • Boston • San Francisco • Toronto • Sydney • Auckland • Singapore • Hong Kong
Tokyo • Seoul • Taipei • New Delhi • Cape Town • São Paulo • Mexico City • Madrid • Amsterdam • Munich • Paris • Milan

PEARSON EDUCATION LIMITED

Edinburgh Gate
Harlow CM20 2JE
United Kingdom
Tel: +44 (0)1279 623623
Web: www.pearson.com/uk

First edition published 2016 (print and electronic)
© Pearson Education 2016 (print and electronic)

The right Kerrie Fleming to be identified as authors of this work has been
asserted by her in accordance with the Copyright, Designs and Patents
Act 1988.

ISBN: 978–1-292–08304–9 (print)
   978–1-292–08306–3 (PDF)
   978–1-292–08305–6 (eText)
   978–1-292–08307–0 (ePub)

British Library Cataloguing-in-Publication Data
A catalogue record for the print edition is available from the British Library

Library of Congress Cataloging-in-Publication Data
Fleming, Kerrie.
  The leader's guide to emotional agility : how to use soft skills to get hard
results / Kerrie Fleming. 1 Edition.
    pages cm
  Includes bibliographical references and index.
  ISBN 978-1-292-08304-9 (pbk.)
  1. Leadership. 2. Emotions. I. Title.
  BF637.L4F584 2016
  658.4'092019--dc23
                                   2015035058

10 9 8 7 6 5 4 3 2 1
19 18 17 16 15

Print edition typeset in 9pt Melior Com by SPi Global
Print edition printed by Ashford Colour Press Ltd, Gosport

NOTE THAT ANY PAGE CROSS REFERENCES REFER TO THE PRINT
EDITION

The departed leader has left an imprint of great magnitude.

Contents

About the author

Dr Kerrie Fleming is a faculty member of Ashridge Executive Education at Hult International Business School where she specialises in leadership development with particular expertise in the field of leader emotional intelligence (EI) and its practical application for individuals and organisations.

Kerrie is a client and program director and has designed and delivered customised, MBA and open leadership and management development programs for senior executives for international and indigenous Fortune 500 companies across the UK, Europe and the Middle East. Prior to working in executive education, Kerrie worked as a university lecturer teaching strategy, management, economics and marketing and previously worked in the areas of strategic acquisition management, account management and customer service with a large multi-national food organisation.

Kerrie has co-authored a chapter with Dr David Caruso in *The Conceptions of Leadership* by Goethals *et al.* and is co-editor of the forthcoming book *Inspiring Leadership* by Fleming and Delves. She is an invited speaker at business events, has featured on BBC Radio and is a regular contributor to HR and learning and development practitioner publications. She is a reviewer for *The International Journal of Human Resource Management* and has presented and chaired many sessions at international conferences. She is the convener of the 8th Annual 'Developing Leadership Capacity Conference' at Ashridge Business School in 2016.

Acknowledgements

Ashridge is a historic and inspiring place where we meet the most interesting (and endearing) executives who take the time to try to become more effective in their leadership practice. They often arrive in a state of flux and anxiety but leave much calmer, having figured out that they alone are the key to their own success. We are always inspired by those who take the difficult decision to look closely at themselves to understand how they can work with the gifts they inherently have, and use these to lead. It has been my privilege to be part of so many of their journeys, which has helped me fulfil my own leadership journey and contribute to this publication. My colleagues at Ashridge collectively offer a wonderful environment for these executives who hold such responsibility in the management of our global economy. I would like to thank those colleagues for being such magnificent hosts. In particular, Roger Delves, Vicky Vass, Ian Downie, James Moncrieff, Gemma Fesemeyer, Tony Sheehan, Fiona Dent, Mike Brent, Sharon Olivier, Vicki Culpin and a host of colleagues at Ashridge House and beyond for their endless support and comradeship. Special mention to Dr David Caruso at Yale for helping me in the translation of emotional intelligence to help those executives.

For David, Sarah and James, who have finally helped me to make sense of the world.

Publisher's acknowledgements

We are grateful to the following for permission to reproduce copyright material:

Figure 8.1 courtesy of Karen N. Caruso; figure 11.2 from Levitt, T., 'Exploit the business life cycle', *Harvard Business Review*, 1969, reprinted courtesy of Harvard Business School Publishing; figure 11.3 from Bridges, W., *Managing Transitions: Making the Most of Change,* Nicholas Brealey Publishing, 2009. UK and Commonwealth rights granted by Nicholas Brealey Publishing; other rights by permission of Da Capo Press, a member of The Perseus Books Group.

All *Financial Times* articles © The Financial Times Limited. All Rights Reserved.

Why you need to read this book

▌ It examines the key challenges that you as leader face as you compete in highly complex and global environments. It offers suggestions for developing and leveraging your real self to overcome these challenges.

▌ It offers seven step-by-step strategies on how to increase your emotional agility as leader using the medium of emotional intelligence.

▌ It examines your self-awareness and that of others, and outlines tactics on how to perceive and acknowledge emotions objectively to improve your leadership practice.

▌ It provides insight into the behaviours of you and your team and how to understand what is behind the emotion you are experiencing so that you can manage any emotional output more effectively.

▌ It will help you acknowledge and appreciate emotions as they arise and learn effective strategies on how to manage your emotions to increase your own emotional agility and resilience.

▌ It offers strategies that you can adopt to manage the emotions of others and make emotionally agile judgements on how to tackle certain situations.

▌ It will explore mindfulness as a strategy for increasing your emotional agility and your resilience.

▌ It offers some skills on how to improve your performance management abilities in performance management, build high-performing and creative teams, while understanding yourself and leading your team in an emotionally agile manner.

Introduction

This book offers seven easy steps on how to develop your emotional agility to increase leadership impact. Emotional agility (EA) is a term coined by Susan David and Christina Congleton in the *Harvard Business Review* (November 2013); they describe it as 'the ability to attend to and use one's inner experiences (both good and bad) in a more mindful, productive way'. It is akin to emotional intelligence (EI) in action. EI has been linked to better emotional health, reduction of bullying in schools, creativity, high-performing teams, transformational leadership and innovation. EA, although in its infancy in business contexts, has been demonstrated to help people alleviate stress, reduce errors, become more innovative and improve job performance. The popularity of both concepts abounds, as a simple Google search on the topic of emotional intelligence (EI) currently throws up over nine million entries on the topic, while a similar search for emotional agility (EA) offers over three million entries.

Structure of the book

This book is evidence-based, reflecting the management experience, research findings and work on the development and delivery of leadership programmes to the world's senior executives across a range of industries. The chapters use the Mayer, Salovey and Caruso Emotional Intelligence Test (MSCEIT) blueprint of emotions as a canvas on which to explore emotional agility. They offer real-life illustrations from leaders just like you, facing real challenges and triumphs.

The book is divided into two parts:

▌**Part 1** offers seven steps on how to become a more
emotionally agile leader and features chapters on self-
awareness, awareness of others, using and understanding
emotions and ways to manage emotion in yourself and
in those around you. In order to be the most effective
in your emotional agility, it is useful to follow the steps
chronologically.

▌**Part 2** examines the application of EA during important
role functions such as leading difficult performance
appraisals, motivating a disengaged team, promoting
creativity and innovation and enhancing your leadership
abilities and brand. In the context of leadership, it will
help you embark on a journey of self-discovery and
encourage you to think about who you are and how you
operate as a leader.

Overall, this book offers seven steps on how you can develop
emotional agility and practise it, using real-life examples
within your own leadership journey. It will force you to look
deeper inside yourself to understand what the key values
are that drive you, the implications of this knowledge and
how you can capture and utilise this self-awareness to make
better decisions at work.

The seven steps to emotional agility (EA)

This section offers the reader seven steps on how to become a more emotionally agile leader and recommends some techniques to help build self-awareness and your awareness of others. It also offers a means to help you recognise, use and understand emotions in yourself and others and how to manage these emotions. Each chapter offers a combination of explanations, self-assessment exercises, case studies, reflections and strategies in order to help you put the skills of emotional agility into action. In order to be most effective in your emotional agility, it is useful to follow the steps chronologically as one will lead to the other. It may not be enough to be agile in just one or two steps as it may reduce your overall effectiveness in emotional agility.

Step One: the real you

Be yourself; everyone else is already taken.

Oscar Wilde

The opening questions

▌ What job do you have?

▌ What car do you drive?

▌ How do you like to dress?

▌ How do you like to communicate?

The answers to these questions represent objects that make up the desired impression you wish to create in the world, the cultivation of which begins as early as childhood. Most people strive to enact this persona to fulfil their public image and promote the version of themselves that they wish people to see. This process is normal, but if overdone it can be laborious.

The leaders who have lost their way

As professional consultants and facilitators, some of the clients we meet have adopted a particular image at work for many years and seek help when this no longer works for them professionally. They have lost the ability to influence others, lead their teams and get promoted in their organisations. They know that something needs to change and seek the *magic bullet* that will make this happen so they can slip safely back into continuity. Most request the formula on how to be successful. We tell them that there is no formula, but the answer lies inside themselves. We ask them to think about who they really are and what is important to them. They often discover that their true self is very different from the image of themselves that they have projected publicly over the years.

At Ashridge we use a variety of experiential methods to help our participants uncover their true self, through working through intense simulations, in-depth facilitation, coaching and action-learning. Other providers of similar intensive development include the *Leaders Quest* organisation, which brings senior business leaders to remote and desperately poor parts of the world to explore their leadership and how it can make a difference in the world. During these journeys these leaders to define who they are, their place in the world and their legacy to the world.

The first thing to do is assess your values and understand what is important to you. Values are those (highly subjective) traits or qualities that you deem important and influence how you and others behave. They are deeply held beliefs which typically evolve from childhood influences from family, friends and peers, education and religious and social affiliations. Examples of values might include: respect, quality, efficiency, dignity, compassion, friendliness and optimism. As facilitators, we often have very robust discussions with our participants to understand which values are good and which are bad. The answer is impossible, as everyone holds different and rather subjective opinions about what is right and what is wrong. However, in most societies across the world, there are some legal and moral codes of values that must be upheld in order to prevent anarchy in such societies.

Values and success

Take Tony Hsieh, CEO and founder of Zappos, an online shoe retailer that was bought by Amazon for $1 billion in 2009. He attributes the success of the company to four values which he terms 'PLUR': peace, love, unity and respect. These four values were a consolidation of ten of the team's personal values and, in essence, have become the organisation's objective principles, which are defined as: objective, self-evident, self-validating natural laws which all adhere to. The fact that the whole organisation embraces them means that the binding power of shared values transforms them into super-values, creating not just consolidation but an utterly solid foundation. They seem to be quite unconventional values to build a company, yet they are those that offer the greatest motivation to people to strive towards something they really believe in. As a leader, this passion is very attractive to others as they see you solidly pursuing a vision that is led by a set of key assumptions and beliefs. Most human beings enjoy being led by those they deem competent and trustworthy.

> Most human beings enjoy being led by those they deem competent and trustworthy

Understanding your values will offer you the best information to guide your decision making and reactions as a leader. Aiming to live by those values as much as possible will induce followership, as people respond to those whose words and actions correspond. For this to happen, your work and personal environment must nourish those values in order to avoid emotional angst, which is bad for stress levels both for you and for those around you. It is helpful to identify with a circle or work environment which is aligned to your values so that you become more relaxed and fulfilled in your decision making.

EXERCISE 1.1

What are your values?

List your personal values

_____

_____

_____

_____

Being aware of your values offers clues as to why you behave and react the way you do in certain situations. Our most primal instinct is to defend those values at all costs and being unaware of such reactions can lead to disruption both in yourself and those around you.

EXERCISE 1.2

Meeting someone with different values

▌ Consider a recent situation that provoked a really strong emotional response in you. Let's examine what happened.

▌ Describe the situation/outcome and how you felt.

▌ Can you guess the values of the other party?

▌ How do you think they felt?

EXERCISE 1.3

Understanding our reactions

▌ Now consider Exercise 1.2: which of your personal values were contradicted?

▌ Why were these particular values of such importance to you? Briefly discuss.

▌ Now armed with both sets of values, how could an outcome have been reached that was respectful of both sets of values?

▌ If not, why not?

▌ What could you do differently to change the outcome?

Your emotional response to the world is primitive and
has evolved over thousands of years. Its original function
was to send some very swift and powerful messages to the
body to release some fight or flight hormones so you could
tackle whatever threat was looming in your midst. Although
contemporary threats in most work environments may not be
life endangering, we still retain the same set of evolutionary
reactions to situations that threaten our position or status.
The force of your emotional reaction may not be appropriate
but will happen unconsciously. Therefore, the first part of
becoming more emotionally agile is to pay attention to both
the triggers and your responses. Understanding why you
react the way you do will allow you to catch the emotional
response, watch it arrive and find a way to manage it
appropriately. This will be dealt with throughout the book.

> The force of your emotional reaction
> may not be appropriate but will happen
> unconsciously

CASE STUDY

A strong emotional response at work

Larry had been taught from a young age by his father that
with hard work he could achieve anything. This had finally
paid off as he had recently been promoted to manage a team
of ten engineers in the automotive division of his company,
where he had worked for fifteen years. He was both excited
and daunted by the opportunity. His boss, Jane, said that
she had a strong belief that he could do the job well and set
a series of targets for the first six months. Larry worked out
a comprehensive plan using project management software
and was delighted to see the targets and timelines were very

achievable. The following week, he held a meeting with his team, using a PowerPoint presentation to outline the plan and what the team would need to achieve in the first two, four and six months of the project. The team listened intently. They asked very few questions but seemed to agree with his plan and Larry left the meeting feeling very positive.

A couple of weeks later when Larry checked his project plan and work activity software to ensure that the targets and the timelines were being met, he noticed that there had been no work on the project by any of the team. When he approached the most senior engineer, Jon, and asked him how the new project was going, Jon said that they simply didn't have any time to work on this as they were busy ensuring that all the day-to-day projects were being done. Larry was stunned. He thought he had an agreement with the team and felt very let down. He walked away from the conversation with Jon feeling bewildered but, by the time he reached his desk, he was feeling very annoyed. In fact he was feeling angry towards his team. He wanted to confront each of them and tell them that they were lazy and it was their job to complete this new project. He sat for a while and suddenly started to feel frightened. What if the team didn't complete the project, what would Jane say? Would he lose his promotion? He had received a pay rise for the new role and it was great to have extra money coming in every month. He had promised his family a special holiday next year.

Over the next few days, Larry found himself in a spiral of negative emotions. He thought about going to see Jane to explain that the team were not capable and needed more resources. He thought of suggesting that some members were simply not up to the job and that it was not his fault they would not make the targets. However, he began to feel helpless and despondent. Why had the team let him down? Perhaps it was his management style or maybe the team were trying to destroy his reputation? Deep down he knew he wasn't up to the job. Why had Jane given him the role? She must have known he wouldn't be able to manage such a

> difficult group of people. Maybe, she had set him up to fail so he would lose his job entirely? He spent the next few weeks in his office avoiding both Jane and the team.

Recognise any of this? You may not be an engineer or have a boss called Jane but the spiral of emotions that has just been described may be recognisable to you. Most people keep this chaotic spiral to themselves as they cannot let the world know since it might just confirm all of their fears of worthlessness, inadequacy or incapability. In essence, what feeds this spiral is your emotional response to your adult world, which is often quite childlike in its manifestation. During times of stress and vulnerability, when people start to feel angry, they sometimes take a childlike route to an emotion such as anger, to the only time they really could express the emotion openly and be cajoled back to a better mood by parents or carers. For the most part, people have never developed an adult response to anger that could lead to better outcomes in a work context. However, the good news is that you can hone your responses using emotional agility, simply by watching the emotion happen, becoming aware of it, understanding the cause of the response (i.e. someone contradicting your values) and managing it in a way that is measured and more adult-like. There are a number of theories within modern psychology that can help deepen our understanding of this, and one of these is transactional analysis (TA), which is now briefly explained.

Transactional analysis

TA evolved as a means of explaining the interactions between individuals, and suggests that something called *ego state* underlines every transaction we make with those around us. The creator of TA, Eric Berne, defines *ego state* as a consistent pattern of feeling and experience directly related to a corresponding consistent pattern of behaviour. There are three ego states which we can default into: Parent, Child and Adult.

The Parent represents a massive collection of recordings in the brain of external events experienced or perceived in, approximately, the first five years of life. Since the majority of the external events experienced by a child are actions of the parent, the ego state is named Parent.

The Child, in contrast to the Parent, represents the recordings in the brain of internal events associated with external events the child perceives. Stated another way, stored in the Child are the emotions or feelings that accompany external events. Like the Parent, recordings in the Child occur from childbirth all the way up to the age of, approximately, five years old.

The Adult is the last ego state. Close to one year of age, a child begins to exhibit gross motor activity. The child learns that he or she can grab a toy. In social settings, the child can play hide and seek. This is the beginning of the Adult in the small child. Adult data grows out of the child's ability to see what is different from what he or she observed (Parent) or felt (Child). In other words, the Adult allows the young person to evaluate and validate Child and Parental data. Berne describes the Adult as being 'principally concerned with transforming stimuli into pieces of information, and processing and filing that information on the basis of previous experience'.

When you interact with those around you, especially when an emotional response has been triggered, either because of a contravention to your values or simply an unexplained emotion, you might normally lapse into one of these ego states. An example that Berne cites is as follows:

Agent's Adult: 'Do you know where my cufflinks are?' (Note that this stimulus is directed at the Respondent's Adult).

Respondent's Child: 'You always blame me for everything!'

In order to elicit the best possible outcome from this situation it may have been more helpful for the Respondent to reply in Adult as follows:

Respondent's Adult: 'I think they're on the desk.'

Such a simple example offers some insight into the way you often react to fairly straightforward interactions, leading to suboptimal outcomes. When you respond in Adult, it usually means you have thought through the response in a reasonable and independent way. When you respond in Parent you are responding in the way in which your carers would, which often isn't reflective of who you are now. When you respond in Child you are immediately responding, using feelings, which isn't always the healthiest approach to achieving a good outcome. An adult-like response is what builds leadership ability as people will start to trust your responses as calm and measured as opposed to reactionary and unpredictable. Thomas Harris has written extensively on this in a popular book called *I'm OK – You're OK*. The theory of TA, combined with knowledge of your values, can help you to begin to figure out who you really are and how you can begin to live in the world as an adult. This will ensure that your journey into leadership will not be hijacked by your Child ego state when things go wrong.

> Our adult-like response is what builds leadership ability

IN SUMMARY

This chapter, its content, exercises and case study are an excellent starting point to help you develop a deeper understanding of who you are and your inherent drivers. Knowing your values is the key to understanding why certain situations provoke severe emotional reactions in you. Later chapters will help you to pick up on these reactions earlier, understand and manage them.

At this stage you should now:

▌ have started your journey to becoming more self aware

▌ be aware of your own values

▌ understand how these values define and shape how you behave and why

▌ notice the strength of your response, when your values are contradicted by others

▌ understand the difference and power of an adult versus child response.

Step Two: how do you feel and why does it matter?

He to whom. . . emotion is a stranger, who can no longer pause to wonder and stand rapt in awe, is as good as dead: his eyes are closed.

Albert Einstein

Notice any feelings?

When was the last time you felt angry? I mean real anger. A time when you were so annoyed that you wanted to scream or break something just to hear the sound of it crashing to the ground and feel a little bit better? The Greek concept of *kefi* (high spirits and fun) encourages the smashing of plates, most commonly at wedding receptions, when it is said to symbolise good luck and a happy and lasting marriage. Building on this symbolic activity, a popular Greek restaurant in London encourages its diners to smash plates after dinner, describing the practice as one that also releases an individual's stress. Perhaps you haven't felt anger in a long time? Your role in life and work may force you to remain poised and in control at all times. Perhaps you have become an expert at pushing away such unhelpful emotions and encouraging those around you to do the same? You can lead a team without much passion or conviction because it is safer to stay in a state of measured calm than lurch from one emotion to the other, which you see as unhelpful. Being calm and considered is a good thing but only if it is supported by real and acknowledged feelings underneath. Otherwise, it is a calm denial of the real rollercoaster of emotions that most humans experience all of the time.

CASE STUDY

Not knowing how one is feeling

Sarah worked in a government strategy office. She took her job very seriously and was proud of the fact that she played a small part in the writing and publication of public policy. She had worked hard at school and university and was successful working in a well-paid job of great status which impressed her family, who had high ambitions for her. Her life growing up had been an orderly and sensible affair in which her family managed any difficulties with great poise and silence.

As the years passed, Sarah realised that all of the ambitions she had had since she was young had now been realised and she momentarily felt very proud of herself. She basked in her achievements, but over time something niggled at her. She couldn't quite tell what it was but this uncomfortable sensation just wouldn't leave her. . . In her role she managed a small team, who were reasonably efficient, but there was one team member, Megan, who was always bringing her personal problems to work. Sarah found it most inappropriate and frowned upon such behaviour. She felt it was her duty to ensure that Megan did her job quietly and stopped disturbing the team with her latest drama.

Sarah decided to tackle the problem and informed Megan to get on with her job and stop bringing her personal issues into the workplace. She told Megan that she had a serious and responsible job to do and, if she didn't stop her nonsense, Sarah would report her behaviour to the senior manager. Megan became very upset and stormed out of the meeting crying, loudly declaring that Sarah was a cold boss and nobody liked her anyway. Sarah was shocked and annoyed. She immediately went to her senior manager and reported the situation but didn't receive the response she had hoped for. Her boss suggested that she spend more time listening to her team and understanding how she could be more supportive, as she had had similar complaints about Sarah in the past.

Sarah was stunned as she left the meeting. The uncomfortable sensation that had been niggling at her flooded back into her body. She couldn't understand what had just happened. Surely she was the person who was right in this situation? How could they say she was a cold person? Was she cold? How did she feel? She honestly didn't know as it had been so long since she had felt anything. It was unsettling. She went to the local café and ordered a large slice of cake. She ate it with relish and immediately felt much better.

The case study above offers a good example of someone who is repressing emotions in order to stay in control. This is fine for a short period of time but most human beings are emotional creatures who regularly experience emotions that infiltrate their actions and decision-making ability. To revisit transactional analysis (TA), Sarah was behaving in Parent state towards Megan and Megan responded in Child state. Sarah's boss's reaction was firmly in Adult state, but Sarah took the news in her Child ego state. Sarah's way of behaving throughout her life to date had been in Child state as her main aim was to please her parents and now her boss. She hadn't really figured out what it was that she wanted to do as an independent adult. This was, perhaps, what was lying behind the emotions she was experiencing, which simply would not leave her. Until Sarah acknowledges who she really wants to be as a free-thinking independent adult, she will continue to face the situations described above. She will also start to notice that the behaviours which she has previously been rewarded for are no longer useful in the organisation she works for, which seems to value a caring and compassionate approach. This may be something strange and alien to her but, unless she listens and starts to practise this behaviour, she will find herself isolated and unpopular.

Working with feeling beings

It would be very useful if managers could hire people who could park all of their emotions upon their arrival at work so they could focus solely on the job that they have been hired to do. However, this would be akin to hiring a robot to do the job. One must remember that people are simple creatures with physiological and emotional needs. These needs never leave them. Even when organisations require people to work from 9 am to 5 pm using their cognitive function, people cannot switch off their emotional needs. For the most part, modern organisations are just physical environments that house people to get on with the assigned task. However, in spite of providing shelter, warmth and food at work, emotional needs inevitably start to surface, and most organisations don't know how to cope with them. Some build large human resource departments to deal with the messy business of people being unhappy, while others offer external counselling services (helpline telephone numbers often listed discreetly on the back of lavatory doors). The behaviour that is rewarded and recognised in most organisations is cognitive function, i.e. the ability to be logical, efficient, to work with complexity and data to solve problems. In fact, most performance management systems are designed to measure people's success by using metrics to quantify output. If you fail the metrics, then you are not up to the task or fail to be one of the team. Unfortunately, the most efficient performers and the brightest can lose their expertise if their rationality is disrupted when something affects their emotional state. It can be a minor tweak of someone contravening their values or it can be a major life-changing event such as the death of a family member, divorce or an illness that halts cognitive function. Organisations often respond in one of two ways. They quietly push the person aside and replace them with someone who is functioning cognitively or offer support to help the person rebuild their emotional self and return to full cognitive functioning to achieve the job that they are paid to do.

> Emotions are legitimate states and are helpful and powerful sources of data

The key point is that emotions are legitimate states and are, in fact, helpful and powerful sources of data to help people live their lives in a way that is balanced and fulfilling. In our work with leaders we often meet the brightest minds but the saddest hearts. I have sat with some fantastically successful people who are deeply unhappy, wishing for a simpler existence. These executives find themselves in a cul-de-sac as they have built a complex and expensive existence around their public self. Eventually, the tide of emotion, which they have held back for so long, engulfs them and often leaves them helpless wrecks with no way out. To help avoid such experiences, you can start to become aware of emotions as they appear. It is not about becoming an emotional mess where you spend all day thinking about how you feel and telling everyone – it is quite the opposite. In TA terms, this is about managing contamination of our Adult ego state, and accessing the emotional Child through the thoughtful Adult. Recognising emotions has been proven to help you make better decisions and become a better leader. To help us with this, it is good to recognise what types of emotions we can experience as human beings.

Types of emotions

While this book examines emotions and their importance within your context as a leader in business, there has also been a plethora of scientific research to help us understand what emotions are and how they emerge. It might be useful to make a foray into the science here. There are two aspects to understanding emotions. The first is a list of *basic emotions,* which include ten discrete emotions: fear, anger, enjoyment, disgust, interest, surprise, contempt, shame, sadness and guilt (Izard, 2009). There are a further six emotion categories – relief, fear, hurt, bitterness, disappointment and worry (Shaver, Schwartz and Wu, 1992) – while Fisher (1997) lists thirteen emotions: affection, pleasure, happiness, pride, optimism, enthusiasm, frustration, anger, disgust, unhappiness, disappointment, embarrassment and worry. The number of emotions seems quite extensive but is, in fact, finite. The second aspect of emotions is *emotion schemas,* which are dynamic emotion–cognition interactions, or how your situational responses emerge over time. This basically means that how people utilise their emotions is dependent on emotion–cognition interaction, which occurs partly from experiencing the emotion, and partly from learned cognitive, social and behavioural skills (Izard, 2009). Similar to the TA ego states, you might experience a combination of these depending on whether you respond in Adult, Parent or Child state. This response is also closely connected to the evolution of your values, which we described in Step One, and to your learned response to emotions.

Our reactions to emotions

The academic literature suggests that people can have three types of reactions to an emotion:

1. **Conscious cognitive process** occurs when empathy is expressed toward the person displaying the emotion.

2. **Conditioned or unconditioned emotional response** is more common, and is based on prior or similar

emotional experiences. For example, as a child you
will have learned what anger looks like from watching
those who were around you. If your parents or carers
raised their voices and shouted abuse at each other over
whose turn it was to take out the garbage, this will be
your experience of what anger is supposed to look like.
On the other hand, if you grew up in an environment
where there was no row about this chore but the affected
spouse went about it sulkily but silently, that is what
anger might look like for you. These events will become
the norm for how you behave when you feel a similar
emotion.

3. **Mimicry/feedback** is where followers mimic the person
expressing the emotion (Hatfield *et al.*, 1994).

All of these emotions, schemas and responses will influence
how you think, feel and behave, which has a huge impact on
how people respond to you as a leader. A learned response
to emotions as a child is a pretty hopeless response in an
adult and in particular in a leadership context. In order
to be most effective, it is encouraged that you recognise
the emotions when they occur so that you can understand
their triggers and background. You can then evoke the most
effective response both in yourself and in others.

EXERCISE 2.1

Think about when you felt. . .

Let's start by exploring a time when you (a) experienced an
emotion, (b) the memory, (c) the physical sensations, (d) the
trigger, (e) the outcome and your overall reflections. This may
not be something that comes easily to you, but try with one
emotion that is more recent and recognisable.

Primary emotion	When you last felt this emotion	What happened to you physically – describe the sensations	Trigger event or person	What was the outcome?	If this was triggered again would you respond differently?
Joy					
Trust					
Fear					
Surprise					
Sadness					
Anticipation					
Anger					
Disgust					

observational skills and a deep understanding of yourself and others. An example of this could be a team member who has been tasked with a new project and feels overwhelmed by it. They may experience some initial apprehension at the challenge of being able to complete the task well. Apprehension can be described as an anxiety or fear that something bad will happen. If they don't communicate this emotion and you as their leader don't see it, then, if left unrecognised or unmanaged, it will move into the next stage of the Plutchik Wheel, which is fear. Fear may now encourage a whole new set of behaviours by the team member, which might include blaming others for their inefficiencies, zero progress or defensiveness. If this still isn't tackled by the leader, the next and most intense form of this emotion that will emerge is terror. This is when the brain is completely hijacked by the emotion and not only will the project fail but this person may do something quite unpredictable as a result of feeling this emotion.

EXERCISE 2.2

Let's practise recognising an emotion

▌ What is the difference between apprehension and anticipation? Can you think about how they are different?

▌ Let's now examine the emotion of apprehension. When was the last time you felt apprehensive?

▌ How did you know you felt that way?

▌ Did you feel a sensation in your body? Were you hot or cold?

▌ What made you feel this way?

▌ What happened next?

▌ Did you go deeper into the emotion and if so why? Or did you start to shift away from the emotion and feel more positive?

▌ What have you learnt about yourself from this experience?

How to notice feelings

As a leader, it is very important to develop a skill set that allows you to perceive those less intense emotions. In Step One, when explaining why people respond the way they do, it was suggested that the evolutionary part of your brain is triggered if your homeostasis state thinks that there may be some danger and forces you to assess the situation and respond by freeze, fight or flight. This danger may not be life-threatening but something deep in your body is warning you to pay attention even to this slightest sensation. It is possible that something or someone is contravening your values, those of your organisation, or indeed the culture you have created, that you want to maintain and protect within your team. In order to handle this message in an Adult ego state, you must listen carefully to your physiological response and utilise this information to help you make an optimal decision.

> You must listen carefully to your physiological response

What is going on in your body?

You can pause, feel the sensations (often in your stomach region) and reflect on what or who is triggering this response. Your subsequent actions can help to change this response, either by deepening it or shifting it into a different one. This takes practice and lots of reflection. Step Seven will look at some techniques that can help you to use the medium of mindfulness to manage this exact process. If you are still struggling to understand what emotions actually feel like, you can pay attention to the physical sensations that are happening in the body when you feel a particular emotion. For example, when you feel fearful you may experience a cold sensation around your body, when you feel angry you might become physically hot or when happy you might feel warm inside. These are quite easy clues to help you pick up emotions as they are happening. Your decision-making processes as a leader can be much improved by simply paying attention to what is going on inside your body. This will offer you some powerful clues as to whether you are on the right track or have in fact strayed into some danger as you see it. If you can become skilled at picking up the emotion early, you can help manage it before it evolves into something deeper, such as rage, which can be an inappropriate emotion to display in the incorrect context. In the Case Study earlier, if Sarah begins to pay attention to the *niggling* sensation, she might find that her body is so exhausted from being in control that there are some emotional leakages that are trying to gently bring her attention to how she is operating either in her Parent or Child ego state.

EXERCISE 2.3

Some activities to help you tune into your feelings

▌ Select a piece of music that evokes a happy or a sad memory.

▌ Be aware of the sensations in your body as you hear the music and re-immerse yourself in the memory. (This schema will send you momentarily back into the moment you heard the music, who was with you and the context in great and vivid detail.)

EXERCISE 2.4

Some more activities to help you tune into your feelings

▌ Walk through an art gallery and find a painting that is so evocative it stops you in your tracks and you simply have to study it.

▌ Examine what is happening to you physiologically and now reflect on why that's the case.

▌ What emotion are you experiencing?

▌ Can you let the emotion flow through your body or are you stopping it because it feels unnatural?

These simple exercises are small but very effective in understanding how you feel and how it can impact your decision-making abilities as a leader.

IN SUMMARY

How you feel is an important piece of knowledge to have. You should now understand that feelings are an inevitable part of your physiological make-up and, no matter how efficient you are at controlling them, they will always appear in some form. This chapter offers you some useful activities to help you tune into and start to feel your emotions, label them and change them if needed. It is important to point out that you are responsible for your emotions and, no different from owning an unruly pet, you have to take responsibility for how they manifest. Being emotionally agile means that you become aware of getting angry but you can now either choose to continue on that emotional course, or stop, challenge and change it. Same with envy, or even love. This idea of taking responsibility, which is also central to the Adult state in TA terms, is a fundamental thing for you as a leader to grasp. Without it you can be powerful but emotionally incontinent. This step offers you the skills to assess these emotions as they arise and subsequent chapters will offer some insight into how to deal with them for the best outcome for you as leader.

Step Three: becoming aware of others

Far from interfering with rationality, the absence of emotion and feeling can break down rationality and make wise decision making almost impossible.

Damasio

CASE STUDY

The manager who never noticed

Dave, a senior IT manager, arrives at his office following his usual commute to work. It has been a tough journey with lots of traffic and he is feeling a bit tired as he didn't sleep last night. Dave really needs a cup of coffee before he gets to his desk but needs to check his smartphone to see what time his first meeting starts. He is actually quite gifted at being able to gaze into his mobile phone and walk towards his office at the same time. There is something so comforting and familiar about scrolling through his phone. It feels almost like he is enveloped in a cloak of invisibility for a while and doesn't have to make eye contact with anyone for just a little longer. Most of Dave's team are at their desks already. They watch him come in, same thing every morning, walking zombie-like, staring into his phone, completely oblivious to the fact that some of his team have actually been in since 7.30 am. One of the team members in particular, James, is feeling annoyed. He has been working very hard the last few months and nobody has noticed, especially Dave. He was sure that all this effort with early mornings and late nights would make a big difference to his promotion application, which is due next week, but it looks like Dave has zero interest, as he never asks about his effort or even says thank you. Maybe he shouldn't bother submitting the application as he doesn't want to make a fool of himself in front of the team if he doesn't get the promotion. In fact, he is sick of this place and being badly treated. He is really good at his job and was top of his class at university. Maybe it's time for him to go to an organisation where he is valued and appreciated. He feels slightly better and logs onto a job-seeker website and registers his details. He should find a new job in no time! In the meantime, Dave is drinking his coffee with the door of his office closed as he needs to concentrate to prepare for his next meeting, which involves presenting a new project to his boss that will yield huge dividends for the company. He is hoping that his best team member, James, will lead it. That guy sure works hard. Dave makes a mental note that he should tell him at his next appraisal in a few months' time, just to keep him motivated and show that he is, in fact, appreciated.

This scenario is all too familiar in workplaces around the globe. The drudgery of work can turn us into vacuous human beings who only interact with each other when there is a business necessity. Through our work in leadership development and teaching, we meet people like Dave on a regular basis. By the time he reaches us, he is usually moaning about how ineffective his team are and how difficult they are. When we ask questions about how the members of their team might be feeling, there is some confusion. Why should this matter? 'There is a job to be done and they just need to get on and do it' is often the answer. The simple reality is that your job as a leader is not only to figure out how to run your business but also to ensure that your team are in a frame of mind to make this happen. The most comprehensive strategies, often formulated in the glossy upstairs boardrooms, and rolled out with great enthusiasm, often fail as those who can make the strategy a success are not engaged with it. They have not been consulted or simply are too entrenched in their own worries to care much about what the star-studded and amazing strategy proposition will do for the organisation.

Pay attention

In order to engage your team, you must first notice what is going on with them collectively and individually. This is easy. When you arrive in your office or a meeting, look around you and observe what is happening. Where and how are people sitting? When Dave arrives at work, he makes the classic mistake of not paying attention to the most important resource he has, his team. Examining his own mood prior to arriving in the office will help Dave enormously as he can then manage it accordingly so that he can focus on his team and their needs. Of course he also needs to ensure that his management priorities are met, but without his team's support he will not have any resources to lead this new project. James may be behaving in Child ego state but his feelings are legitimate and do need to be managed. The easiest way for this to happen is for Dave to work harder at building his relationships with the team, which will encourage James to approach him more readily. Dave can then spot the emotion at its least intense on the Plutchik Wheel of Emotion (Figure 2.1) before it sends James into the spiral of negativity that he is now in.

Always look around you when you are navigating the workplace. The Chief Operations Officer of Facebook, Cheryl Sandberg, wrote a book called *Lean In*, which encouraged women in business to have their say in the workplace environment. The title of her book emerged from observing the dynamics of a busy senior board meeting where all the women sat on chairs at the back of the room, while all the men took their seats at the table. Sandberg's acute observation allowed her to gain some real understanding of the dynamics that play out in boardrooms all over the world and prompted her to write the book. If you are really interested in what is going on and cannot glean the mood from the physical dynamics, you can ask non-agenda questions, which help you ascertain the mood of the room before you launch into the intricacies of the meeting. Examples of these types of questions might include: How was your weekend? How are you doing? What is going well for you? How is project X coming along? What do you think about what happened last week?

> Ascertain the mood of the room before you launch into the intricacies of the meeting

Emotional displays

However, it is important to remember that people display emotions in different ways. Similar to the emotion schemas from the last chapter, everyone has different variations of how they express happiness, sadness, anger, etc. Everyone has a resting face, especially when they feel relaxed. For some people, this resting or baseline expression can look neutral, bored or scathing. They may not feel any of these things but those looking on can make extraordinary assumptions based on this expression. For example, we once worked with a group of European executives on how to increase and improve their influencing skills. As part of the process, we secretly assigned one individual to each member of the group and asked them to quietly observe the other's facial expressions and outward behaviours for the week. They had to gather this data and report back to the person they were observing at the end of the week. One of the participants was informed by her observer that she looked absolutely bored and disinterested for the whole week and, as a result, those who were enjoying the programme avoided her as they felt that she was negative. When the observed participant heard this assertion, she was appalled. She had experienced one of the most engaging weeks of her life and was very shocked that her expression suggested otherwise. She reflected, and decided her primary concern was the impact of her emotional displays on her team. She began to understand why she was not often approached by team members. This feedback began her journey of self-awareness, then working with a coach significantly improved her personal impact.

> People display emotions in different ways

The iceberg

The biggest lesson from all of this is to realise that figuring out how someone is feeling is not achieved by reading facial expression or body language alone. They are only tiny clues and, as seen from the example above, are often highly inaccurate. If you know your team pretty well, then you will recognise their normal demeanour when things are going well and, when they stray from this, you can quickly spot what might be going on. When you don't know people, it may be hard to make comparisons, but you can watch out for body language, tone, eye contact, demeanour and attitude, along with assessing how the conversation is going. Is the person open in their conversation or closed and uninterested? What are the hooks that can re-engage them and build trust with them? There are a number of tools that can be used to build an understanding of what might be going on for those in your teams. Let's now examine two of the most relevant to assist with your emotional agility.

1 The Johari Window

The first tool which will help with understanding other
people and their emotions is the Johari Window (Luft and
Ingham, 1955). This is a simple, well-established and useful
tool for illustrating and improving self-awareness and
mutual understanding between individuals within a group.
It represents information – feelings, experience, views,
attitudes, skills, intentions, motivation, etc. – within or about
a person, in relation to their group, from four perspectives.
These four perspectives are called 'areas' and are as follows:

	Known to self	Not known to self
Known to others	Arena	Blind spot
Not known to others	Façade	Unknown

FIGURE 3.1 The Johari Window

Source: Luft, J. and Ingham, H., 'The Johari Window: a graphic model of interpersonal
awareness'. *Proceedings of the Western Training Laboratory in Group Development* (Los
Angeles: University of California).

The model works using four area quadrants.

1. **Arena or open area**: anything you know about yourself
   and are willing to share is part of your open area.
   Individuals can build trust between themselves by
   disclosing information to others and learning about
   others from the information they, in turn, disclose about
   themselves. This might have happened in the earlier Case
   Study if Dave shared his worries about the upcoming
   presentation with James. He might find that James shared

his worries or indeed could help Dave prepare for the upcoming meeting.

2. **Blind spot area**: any aspect that you do not know about yourself, but others within the group have become aware of, is in your blind area. With the help of feedback from others you can become aware of some of your positive and negative traits, as perceived by others, and overcome some of the personal issues that may be inhibiting your personal or group dynamics within the team. Within the earlier Case Study, Dave's blind spot may be his inability to notice anyone else's feelings in the office. By eliciting feedback, he might gain some insight into how he could employ strategies to work on this.

3. **Façade or hidden area**: there are aspects about yourself that you are aware of but might not want others to know; this quadrant is known as your hidden area. Dave may not want people to know that he is a raging introvert and is very much out of his comfort zone in this role. He worries that people knowing this might undermine his authority and credibility so he hides it beneath behaviours such as checking his smartphone or closing the door of his office.

4. **Unknown area**: this is the area that is unknown to you or anyone else.

How to use the Johari Window

The main aim of the Johari Window is to enlarge the open area, without disclosing information that is too personal. The open area is the most important quadrant, as generally the more your people know about each other, the more productive, cooperative and effective they will be when working together. When you enlarge the open area quadrant. This is often called self-disclosure and it subsequently becomes a give-and-take process that takes place between yourself and the people that you're interacting with. You might want to share with someone an aspect of your life that you had previously kept hidden, such as the fact that you are not comfortable contributing ideas in large groups. This would increase your open area and decrease your hidden area. You can increase your open area by asking for feedback from people. When feedback is given honestly to you, it can reduce the size of your blind area. Sometimes you don't realise these aspects of your character until they are pointed out. By working with others, it is possible for you to discover aspects that you have never understood or been aware of before.

EXERCISE 3.1

Using the Johari Window to help you pick up the emotions of others

Remember the previous situation you described in Exercise 1.2. Reflect on what might lie behind the other person's hidden area of the Johari Window.

▌ Can you guess how they might have felt? What did you notice in their open areas?

▌ On reflection, were there any specific behaviours that were evident prior to the intervention that might have helped you manage the outcome differently? What are their blind areas?

▌ Can you now plot members of your team using the Johari Window?

▌ How many of your team have offered insight into the hidden area of their Johari Window?

---

2 The mood meter

The second tool that will help increase your understanding of emotions is the mood meter, adapted from Russell (1980). Once you have developed your awareness and identified the emotion you can then work with the mood to either change it or utilise it in the best possible way. The mood meter plots and harnesses the mood of individuals or teams using the relationship between feeling and levels of arousal or energy. Russell describes arousal (energy) as high or low and feelings as pleasant or unpleasant. These descriptors are somewhat bland but will make sense once the quadrants are used to demonstrate the mood that emerges when we combine energy and emotion at different levels.

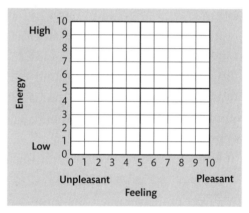

FIGURE 3.2 The mood meter

Source: Adapted from Russell, J. A., 'A circumplex model of affect', *The Journal of Personality and Social Psychology*, 39, 1161–1178, 1980.

EXERCISE 3.2

Plot yourself on the mood meter

▌ How are you feeling on a scale from 0 to 10, 0 being unpleasant and 10 being pleasant? Now plot your number on the mood meter.

▌ How energetic are you feeling right now? Zero means you have low energy and 10 means you have high levels of energy. Now plot your second number on the mood meter.

Your position should appear in one of the quadrants, which we will now evaluate. According to the relationship between feeling and energy, the mood meter suggests that, when we are feeling a certain way and have a certain amount of energy, we will be more inclined to adopt some of the following activities.

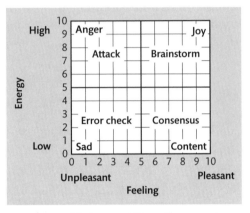

FIGURE 3.3 Plot yourself on the mood meter

Source: Adapted from Russell, J. A., 'A circumplex model of affect', *The Journal of Personality and Social Psychology*, 39, 1161–1178, 1980.

When you are high in energy and feel unpleasant, the result (in the top left-hand quadrant) suggests that you may be prone to attack as the emotion associated with this state is anger. If you are still high in energy and feeling pleasant, this serves to create the emotion joy, which is conducive to brainstorming activity. Research suggests that innovation and creativity happen when people are free from worries and feel joyful and happy. There are, of course, exceptions to this, as seen from famous paintings that were created when the artist had experienced extreme sorrow or heartbreak. When people are low in energy and unpleasant in feeling, this sadness can be a very useful time to carry out more sombre tasks such as error checking or forensic-type activity where they are on the hunt for mistakes. This is useful knowledge, as some leaders often dismiss low-energy team members as being hopeless, when in fact they can utilise their tendency or long-term mood to engage them in a particular activity that might be useful for the business.

The bottom right-hand quadrant, when feeling is pleasant but energy is low, is important when you want to achieve consensus. During our teaching and consultancy in emotional intelligence, we often plot the mood of the group using the mood meter. It is a fun way to see what the collective mood is like and how we can change it, if necessary. For example, if the group suggest that their collective mood is in the top right-hand quadrant (brainstorm), it may be a very useful time for them to get started on a new project and explore some ideas together.

The mood meter is a fun way to see what the collective mood is like

Using the mood meter with your team

The mood meter offers a powerful means to ensure that you stop and assess the mood before you plough on with your agenda. We often meet and observe executives who walk into a meeting room with their teams and immediately launch into the items on the top of the agenda. It is, of course, an efficient way to operate but often entirely ineffective. A diverse group of people sitting in the room may harbour a whole series of feelings and expectations and, unless you try to read the mood or bring the group into the room, you are often wasting your time. Experience suggests that most people, particularly in Western society, politely nod and appear to agree with your agenda but will not take it anywhere beyond the meeting. So, you can try opening the meeting with a question or something that will bring people's attention to the room and find a way for them to relax into a mood that will allow you to get what you want from the meeting. Such questions might include: How are you all doing today? Who would like some coffee before we start?

One participant from the public health sector, who attended an influencing programme at Ashridge, described how stressed her team were as they were operating with few resources and poor pay and conditions. However, this manager really values their work and always tries to inject some appreciation and humour to alleviate the situation. Every Friday at lunchtime, she organises fish and chip lunches for her team and they sit around together eating, swapping stories and de-stressing after their busy week. It is one of the most informative and insightful times for her as a leader and she knows that it helps to shift their mood from the top left-hand quadrant to the bottom right-hand quadrant. It is a small but powerful gesture from a leader who understands the need to recognise moods and manage them. It also demonstrates emotional agility in action and keeps her team motivated and focused during very harsh working conditions.

CASE STUDY

The impact on business of ignoring emotions

A number of years ago, I worked with a large group of scientists who were being asked to move from their (rather aged) laboratory to a brand new state-of-the-art technology and innovation facility over three hundred miles away. There was much anxiety from the team about the move, and, although the executive team were convinced that this was best for the company as they entered new markets, the technologists were concerned about the impact of the move on their families. The company set up a HR team to answer any questions about the new location and offered help to locate new homes and schools for the technologists. As I met each of the technologists for individual coaching sessions, it became very clear to me that there was a huge state of anxiety that was not going to evaporate any time soon. Some were considering leaving the company as they couldn't face taking their children out of school. When the time came, only half the team moved to the new location and the vision for creating a hub of innovation activity was short-lived, as those who moved spent the first six months settling into their environments and were simply too distracted to be creative. They also lamented the loss of their colleagues who they had worked with for many years and found it difficult to get along with the new young scientists who had taken their places. This company is still trundling along with no new products in the pipeline but with a massive capital cost still eating into the company revenue every year. When I spoke to a member of the executive team, he privately said that the project had been a costly failure, as they had completely underestimated the impact on the business of how the team were feeling following the announcement and move. It was an expensive lesson in the importance of paying attention and giving consideration to the mood of your team when aiming for change or success. The role of understanding the mood of the team prior to, during and post change management is a vital ingredient to success or failure of some projects.

EXERCISE 3.3

Judging the mood of your team

▌ Think of a situation where you failed to influence someone or indeed your whole team.

▌ On reflection, where do you think they were on the mood meter?

▌ Where were you positioned?

▌ Why were the team in that mood?

▌ What could you do differently to change the outcome?

As can be seen from Step Three, recognising the emotions of others is very important within your leadership context. The mood of people at work is directly correlated to how productive or creative they can be and, until you recognise this, you will be continually wondering why strategic plans and great ideas that you want to bring to fruition continue to fail. If you establish deep and meaningful relationships with your people, you will become a lot more agile at spotting particular moods and understanding the drivers that can be tapped into to change the mood accordingly.

> The mood of people at work is directly correlated to how productive or creative they can be

IN SUMMARY

Paying attention is one of the most powerful skills you can have as a leader. It will offer you all sorts of clues as to how your team are behaving – if they are engaged they will carry out whatever tasks you deem suitable or appropriate. It is such a simple strategy but one that is overlooked time and time again. Once you have the data, you can then channel it into some powerful outcomes. Later chapters will help you to gain an understanding of why people behave the way they do and how you can attempt to manage them.

At this stage you should be able to:

▌ assess emotions in yourself

▌ spot some emotional cues in others that may signal a change in attitude or behaviour

▌ understand how to change your own mood and that of others

▌ recognise the impact of the team's mood on organisational outcomes.

Step Four: understanding emotions

Nothing in life is to be feared, it is only to be understood. Now is the time to understand more, so that we may fear less.

Marie Curie

Now that you know how you and others might be feeling and how to harness the mood, the next step is to understand what led to the emotion both in yourself and others. When you become disproportionately enraged in a situation with a difficult member of your team, is there something even more complex going on?

The nuclear emotional response

Peter was managing a big client for his organisation. The client had a high net worth and frequently exerted a great deal of pressure on him. To make things even more difficult, the client contract was up for renewal for the first time in five years and they were broadening their search for a supplier. Peter had a good relationship with the purchasing manager and knew that in order to keep the contract his company would have to increase their quality and service. One of the key people delivering this increased service was his colleague Jennifer, who worked closely with the client and had always had a good relationship with them. As the contracts were being discussed, the client asked Peter and Jennifer to deliver a big project in the next few weeks. Peter was confident that they could but Jennifer was concerned that she had other commitments to her team that had been in the diary for the previous twelve months. Peter knew this but decided to cancel her team meeting which clashed with the needs of the client project. He spoke with her boss, who agreed with him that this client contract was very important and that Jennifer should put this as a priority. Peter was delighted and phoned Jennifer to let her know that this had been decided and she needed to attend to the client project and, as such, her meeting with her team had been cancelled.

Jennifer heard with incredulity that Peter had gone behind her back and cancelled her meeting. She felt massively betrayed by both Peter and her boss and was furious that anyone would do such a thing. She had always been very approachable and was confused as to why Peter hadn't come to her and had a conversation so they could sort something out. She told him so on the phone and he became very defensive. He accused her of not being commercial and neglecting to understand the priorities of the business. He hung up the phone on her as he couldn't deal with what she was saying.

After a few days passed they agreed to meet and Jennifer opened the conversation by asking him why he had done what he did. Peter immediately became defensive and said that he didn't like Jennifer's tone and that he felt bullied. Jennifer was amazed by the strength of the reaction and asked him why he was overreacting so badly. At that point, Peter got up from the conversation and stormed off saying that Jennifer was unprofessional and complained about her to her boss.

The nuclear reaction that Jennifer experienced from Peter was indeed disconcerting but the reality is that she had simply stepped on a trip wire that had triggered a much deeper emotional response from Peter that was disproportionate to the event itself. Peter's behaviour was highly irrational and, in transactional analysis (TA) terms, he acted completely in Child ego state. His ability to listen to any other side of the story besides his own was completely inhibited. In Johari Window terms, he revealed that his blind spot was, in fact, quite large. In order for Jennifer to make sense of the situation, it is now important for her to step back and assess whether she was the problem or if there is something deeper going on with Peter.

What is going on with people?

Understanding emotions in others is a difficult task as people may act out a previously felt emotion that is related to a separate incident. That is why, when you meet the full force of an emotion that far outweighs the trigger, it is worth noting that this may be unrelated to the context you are in. How do you establish this and what do you do about it? Sometimes, understanding a similar situation that provoked an extreme reaction inside of you can help you to understand what emotions are happening in others. In fact, you may have experienced a visceral reaction to a situation that started out in a mild way but provoked a response that was so forceful you lost all reason and ability to stand back from the issue.

EXERCISE 4.1

An extreme reaction from you

Think of a situation that provoked a severe emotional response in you that, in hindsight, was disproportionate to the event that triggered it.

▍ Describe the situation, the context, the other people involved.

▍ What was the overriding emotion?

▍ What happened as a result? What did you do, say?

> ▮ Looking back on the event, can you now think about what else might have been going on that evoked such a response?
>
> ▮ What have you learnt about yourself as a result?

Doing exercises like the one presented above is a very useful way to begin to understand why you behave the way that you do in certain situations. This is also true for the other people we encounter. When you meet a behaviour that seems bizarre or out of character in others, no matter how hurt or admonished you might feel, it is useful to take a step back and ask the question: '*What is really going on here?*' This is real emotional agility in action as you are able to park your response and explore some possibilities as to what lies behind the behaviour.

> ## Park your own response and explore what's really going on

For example, if one of your team (rather out of character) acts quite forcefully at a meeting and adamantly hammers home their views without listening or considering others, it may be useful to take some time after the meeting to see what might really be going on for them. This does not mean that you publicly tackle them in the meeting and bring them down to size, but that you make time for a coffee afterwards and ask some open questions as to how things are going for them generally. This type of activity may not fit with the endlessly busy schedule you have set yourself but is one of the most useful and productive ways to spend your time as a leader. Let's now take some time out to examine why this is so important.

Time out
How do you spend your time as leader?

Some of the managers we meet are completely exhausted from overwork and poor resources. They often complain loudly about the bad decision abilities of their CEO or senior team who have no understanding of what it's like for them to work so hard. When we explore with them what type of work they are doing, they usually admit that they are still doing the same work they did prior to being made manager. They are unwilling to let go of the expertise which the company hired them for, and manage those around them. They see the duties of management as cumbersome, where people and their difficulties get in the way of doing the day job. This is where the unravelling of most managers happens. They will not let go of their expert power. The Centre for Creative Leadership's (CCL) 'Derailment Study' (Van Velsor and Brittain, 1995) found that executives who derailed had a string of successes early on in their careers mostly leveraged from being experts and superior problem solvers in their fields. However, as they climbed up through the organisation, the nature of their job demands changed and some of their early career strengths became their weaknesses. These weaknesses ranged from insensitivity to others, failure to build or delegate to their teams and overdependence on a single mentor or leader.

Is any of this familiar to you?

If so, spending time understanding your team's needs and frustrations (such as the situation illustrated in the Case Study earlier) is profoundly important so you can create and maintain a mood that will allow for optimal performance from your team. In fact, a large proportion of your job as manager or leader is to create an environment where your team are located appropriately on the mood meter (Figure 3.2) so that you can ensure that their cognitive function is free from any emotional hijacks. This will involve a large degree of trust from you, which is often a very difficult thing to evoke if you are unused to not being in control. This control is what helps you to be an effective manager, but as you start to mature into the leadership role you will find yourself having to trust those around you to fulfil their task effectively.

An extreme response that had a deeper cause

Mike had worked in the marketing division at Rapido Tube Systems for eight years. He had a strong team who respected him and worked diligently for the division. He had spent many years with each member of the team figuring out their drivers and motivators and fashioning their ambitions to suit the requirements of the company. Mike had successfully created a high-performing team who trusted him implicitly and had mutual respect for one another. He was reasonably satisfied in his job and enjoyed getting on with what needed to be done. The company recently devised a rather ambitious growth strategy to triple its sales revenue over a period of five years. This could be achieved by either acquisition or exponentially reducing costs in-house. In the past month, Mike was informed by his senior team that a new manager would be arriving to help the division achieve this growth ambition. Mike's response was rather lukewarm but nonetheless he agreed to assist the new manager in whatever was needed.

When the new manager, Jonathan, arrived, the team greeted him with some suspicion but tried to make him feel welcome. Jonathan was an introvert and did not engage with anyone from the team and, for the most part, barely made eye contact with anyone from the moment he arrived. His job was to promote efficiencies, for which he was valued by head office. He set an extraordinary target for the division to achieve by the end of the quarter. Mike was stunned but didn't argue and presented the new demands to the team. They were horrified and said there was no way it could be done. Mike urged them along and said that they would all at least have to try. So they did. Jonathan's target of reducing spend by 12 per cent was achieved and beat previous records of spend reduction by 75 per cent. Mike was proud to inform Jonathan that they were all on track but Jonathan made no overt displays of gratitude and simply moved on and talked about the next quarter.

For some reason, which he couldn't understand, Mike started to feel afraid of Jonathan. It became a preoccupation of his, mulling over the way in which Jonathan managed the meetings, and it also became clear to him that the team, too, were slightly afraid or at least intimidated by Jonathan. Mike became defensive on behalf of his team and started to feel helpless when this new manager was wreaking such emotional havoc amongst his wonderful team. He started to avoid Jonathan and found himself slightly palpitating while in meetings with him. As a means to regain control, he decided to confront Jonathan about the team's excellent performance, stating that he and the team had readily achieved the goals set out. Much to Mike's surprise, Jonathan agreed and suggested that perhaps Mike deserved an increase in salary. Mike was stunned but decided to take advantage of the good mood and asked for some professional development, which Jonathan agreed to. Mike left the meeting feeling good but still irritated by the feeling of sheer discomfort and fear. He decided to sit down with his executive coach to discuss what was going on. When the coach started to explore with him as to why Jonathan was causing him so much upset he couldn't really make sense of it. In fact, when he thought about it, Jonathan had elicited a pay rise for him, which his previous manager hadn't done, and had sent him on a rather exclusive leadership programme which made him the envy of his peers. When they started to examine why Mike was feeling this way, the coach asked him if he could recall any person in the past who had evoked a similar reaction. Mike thought for a moment and said, 'My mother'. He surprised himself with such an answer but, when they began to unravel it, Mike started to realise that Jonathan had very similar traits to his mother and he had been terrified of her while growing up. She demanded a lot from him in terms of achievements and, if he didn't fulfil her ambitions for him, he was studiously ignored for a period of time, which was devastating for him as he was a child who really needed affection and endorsements that he was still a good boy.

Figuring it out

This case study is a really good example of the importance
of understanding what is going on behind an emotion.
A particular feeling that can be very strong and linger for
quite some time can cause huge confusion in the mind.
Mike began to experience uncomfortable sensations as
Jonathan displayed certain behaviours. This reaction was
so strong that it swept him into a state of fear and anxiety
and, ultimately, stopped him from understanding why
he was having such a reaction. What is helpful for you
as leader is to explore the emotion and remember where
you met this emotion previously – this can help you to
unravel the triggers of the emotion. For you personally,
it is useful to understand that you have developed some
automatic responses to certain situations and triggers.

> It is useful to understand that you have
> developed some automatic responses
> to certain situations and triggers

In fact, your brain has built and developed a neural pathway
(that connects one part of the nervous system with another)
that is a preferred path or a default reaction to an event or
trigger driven by the emotional schemas we discussed in
Step Three. It is akin to a number of spider webs woven
across your brain. The more robust the web, the more
easily a memory can be recalled, because there are many
more ways in which to access the web. For Mike, this
web had not been accessed in his adult life so it was more
difficult for him to reach into the pathway to review and
understand his reaction. Others, who regularly experience
this reaction, are drawing on a previous memory for how to
respond. This neural pathway is now an automatic response
mechanism that has usually been developed in childhood.
As you can imagine, this is not a very useful skill to have

when you are working as an adult. It is often completely inappropriate in an adult context. This was clear in the case study, as Mike's fear was hijacking what could have been a good and productive relationship between himself, Jonathan and, indeed, his team. Mike already has some skills in emotional agility as he is very tuned into the needs of his team through observing, listening and ensuring that they are well developed and happy in their tasks. Jonathan knows this and is using Mike as the conduit to build the efficiency that he needs. This is fine in the short term but may become less effective in the long term as the team are relying on Mike to translate the task and protect them from someone whom they see as quite fierce in his ambitions for cost reduction. Jonathan's transient role has ensured that he has never been left in one division of the organisation for very long and has moved on once he has achieved the appropriate cost cutting in each division. His emotional agility may be redundant in his current role but will eventually be required once he meets a situation that doesn't quite have the outcome that he needs. As you can see, emotional agility is not a quick solution but something that if developed, can help you over a period of time to respond better in situations and make decisions based on all the facts about the situation and your default response tendencies. It is a key building block to becoming a strong and sustainable leader.

Learning through emotion

Our neuroscience in leadership work at Ashridge suggests that we can recreate these neural pathways by learning new ways to respond to adult situations. In addition, it has been demonstrated that the most powerful way to acquire new knowledge as an adult is at an emotional level rather than a cognitive level. Waller and Reitz's (2015) research on how to increase the transfer of learning during and after a leadership development programme suggests that if facilitators can create a learning environment that allows for people to experience emotions during their learning experience, they build some new neural pathways or responses to situations that are more appropriate to adult contexts. Ashridge's flagship programme called 'The Leader's Experience' (TLE) uses emotional learning methods through the creation of critical incidents throughout the programme. This evokes strong emotional responses in the participants which are managed carefully by expert facilitators and coaches. The literature on neuroscience in leadership suggests that the stronger the emotion experienced during the learning process the more enhanced its recall is at a later point. However, if you overdo the evocation of emotions then there is a risk of complete amygdala hijack where the body and mind prepare for fight or flight.

> The most powerful way to acquire new knowledge is at an emotional level rather than a cognitive level

EXERCISE 4.2

Reflection: how can we begin to develop some new responses?

There are a number of steps you can take:

- Identify the emotion as it arises inside of you. Can you name it?

- Become aware of your body. You may experience a physiological change like heat or coldness. Sense and feel it happen. Name it.

- Before you open your mouth or react, try to observe silently what is happening to you. This will take superordinate strength on your part.

▌Try to remove yourself from the trigger and change the context of your surroundings. Take a walk or grab a coffee.

▌If you cannot do this, take a few minutes to quietly compose yourself and look for an alternative way to react to the situation.

▌When you are alone, either write down what has happened or examine it in your mind and ask some of the following questions:

- What is it about this situation that has made you react in this way?

- When has this happened before?

- Does it remind you of any episode from childhood? Try to recall in vivid detail if you can.

All of these steps will help you to begin the process of becoming more emotionally agile as you can develop a new response to things that usually trigger an adverse reaction.

IN SUMMARY

This chapter offers you a means to select an alternative response to your emotions as they arise. This is a powerful skill that will outwardly manifest as someone who is measured, calm and thinks carefully and deeply about things before reacting. Incidentally, these are some of the key characteristics of successful leaders. They have developed a wisdom that has evolved from previous years of runaway emotions driving bad decision making, and have now learned to stand back and elicit more measured responses to situations. It takes courage and confidence to have such patience and is an extremely powerful skill to have both as a leader and individual. Becoming emotionally agile involves a huge amount of reflection in order to really understand why you react and behave the way that you do.

▌ Often, emotions are completely out of your control but, if you follow the steps outlined in the previous chapters, then you will be able to identify the emotion in yourself as it arises and in others.

▌ If you can begin to understand why emotions happen in the way that they do, you can then go through the process of managing them in a way that allows for a healthier and happier outcome for you and those around you.

The next chapters deal with how to manage emotions in yourself and others. As you can see from some of the cases that have been outlined, this is a key skill in the steps to becoming more emotionally agile. You can be excellent at identifying emotions in yourself and others, using this information, and even at understanding what is driving the emotion, but if you cannot manage it, then it will simply consume you or the other person and wreak much havoc in its wake.

Step Five: managing your own emotions

Wisdom comes with winters.

Oscar Wilde

Preparing an emotionally agile response

The components of managing your emotions are your immediate response to a provocation and the reaction that may occur later. For some people, their immediate response can be one where they are hijacked by the emotion which sends them head-first into a reaction without thinking. This may be further exacerbated when the other party is adept at manipulation or pushing your buttons and, in transactional analysis (TA) terms, your Child ego state is hooked rather than your Adult ego state. If this is familiar territory to you, let's try to avoid this by preparing for the response:

1. **Two scenarios.** Typically, there are two possible scenarios: you will either know that you are heading into a possibly adverse situation at work or you will suddenly find yourself confronted with a provocation that has come from nowhere.

2. **Prepare yourself.** If you do know that a certain reaction will be triggered then you can prepare for the event. This may involve thinking through the situation before you immerse yourself in it and thinking about the person who

will most likely provoke a response in you. Apply the Johari Window – how much of their open area can you see or, contrarily, their blind spot? This is useful data for you to take with you to the interaction.

3. **Be agile in your response.** Now that you understand that a difference in values or a trigger awakens the Child ego state in you, you can decide to listen much more than usual and ask some open questions at this meeting. This will force you to take a step back as opposed to rushing forward once the situation arises.

4. **Manage yourself in the moment.** This preparation will help you to observe the possible avenues that may normally send you into an emotionally charged frenzy and allow you to observe the emotion as it arises. This will prevent the emotion dragging you down under its force and you can hold or freeze the emotion until later, when it is more appropriate to deal with it.

5. **Acknowledge your mood.** It is worth assessing your mood overall before you embark on any interaction or meeting. A level of frustration with the organisation, your boss or spouse, which is lingering from previous events, will pervade all other unrelated future interactions with others. On a deeper level, you may need to spend time outside of the meeting reflecting on the baggage (such as feelings, automatic responses or emotion schemas) that you permanently carry with you. You can then make a decision on whether you wish to continue to carry this baggage or dispose of it through exploring your Child ego state and the reasons why you have such baggage.

6. **Take time to understand.** How many times have you seen an entirely unreasonable email response from someone to what may have seemed like a straightforward exchange? If you can probe deeper, you will often find that this response is a result of a different frustration.

EXERCISE 5.1

How to prepare for a possibly evocative situation

1. How are you feeling about this forthcoming meeting? Sit quietly and alone. Close your eyes and imagine sitting in the chair across from the attendees. What kind of sensations are you experiencing?

2. Now imagine the meeting going badly, where you are criticised or simply ignored when you request some resources. What feelings start to emerge? If you could do or say anything you wanted, what might that be? Imagine it, say it out loud. Shout it if you need to.

3. Now, imagine it is going well. You are calm and in control. You reason with the difficult person in the room. What are they saying and how are you responding? Look at your hands – are your fists clenched or are you relaxed? If they do become difficult, what might be a good way to ensure that you achieve your outcome? Think it through.

Taking some time to manage your emotions prior to hitting any potential hotspots can be a powerful way to pre-empt a personal emotional outburst. It may seem indulgent but it will also actually help you to create some new neural pathways in the brain that will serve you well when you encounter any similar situations in the future. Think about those members of your team or peers in the past who have lost it. They may have publicly expressed their extreme frustration vehemently and righteously but it hindered them politically in the organisation. It may feel good to say what you really feel in the moment, but the long-term implications can be quite damming, especially if you work in a culture that frowns on such emotional outbursts. However, if such a measured preparation is not possible, when you do suddenly encounter such an event you can find a way to put the emotion on hold until later so you can deal with it in a more appropriate way.

Unlocking your emotions

Some people continually feel and express their emotions. Of course, this is a powerful means of generating self-awareness and comes with both benefits and disadvantages if not managed properly. However, there are some people who simply haven't even experienced an emotion in a long time. If this is the case for you, then there are many strategies that you can adopt to manage your emotions, but the key is to ensure that you don't studiously ignore the emotion or repress it. This is a common feature where people simply turn off their ability to feel anything.

Some people can do this over a long period of their lives. This can also be a learned skill from childhood where something hurt you so profoundly that your mind simply couldn't deal with the emotional pain. Therefore, you closed down your feelings and it ultimately became a permanent shut down. For the most part, people have no idea that they have done this as they have nothing to compare feeling or no feeling with. It is only when something happens that unlocks this store of feelings that they often either become overwhelmed or drown in the lifetime of emotions that they have locked away. Alternatively, when they meet an emotion such as love, they find it so utterly bewitching that it often completely derails them and they become convinced that they will love this person for all eternity. This feeling is so acute, it almost has anaesthetic qualities as the person becomes utterly hijacked. Sounds cynical but the frequency of a first love ending in forever is limited to a lucky few. Most people have to go through the roller coaster of sky-high adoration to rock-bottom heartbreak. This is a useful way for the mind to find a happy and healthy medium of emotional states that will probably be less exciting than the initial adoration but grounded in the practical realities of human fallacies and, if we choose to, will allow us to live our lives companionably with another human being for a sustainable period of time.

Going with the highs and lows

If you have both experienced and managed normal emotional highs and lows in life then you probably have good emotional health. It also suggests that you have the skill to remain poised and calm in leadership situations that will manifest publicly as a reputation for being calm and measured in your responses as leader. For the most part, emotions will happen, so you simply *must* deal with them in the moment or at a later stage. You should not ignore the emotion.

Those who have repressed childhood emotions for prolonged periods of time can sink into depression if something shocking happens in adulthood which their mind should normally be able to cope with. The reason for this is that the body and mind have had enough and confront the person with some physical limitation. They may not be able to leave their house or find themselves having palpitations or panic attacks at random times. These disabilities are usually triggered by levels of deep and prolonged stress where the body has had to work extremely hard to keep the emotion hidden or repressed. This is often the starting point of the healing process as people's physical inability to function usually prompts them to seek help as they are frightened and simply do not know what to do.

> For the most part, emotions will happen, so you simply must deal with them

If you have found yourself in this state, the likelihood is that your doctor will suggest removing yourself from the stress situation, i.e. work, and initially prescribe some mild sedatives or relaxants and advise you to seek some professional counselling that will help you unravel what is going on in your mind. We often meet leaders who have experienced such breakdowns and share their stories quite easily, which they hope will prevent others from reaching the same end.

CASE STUDY

The banker breakdown

Mark was a highly successful banker. He was married with two children and had a very supportive wife and loving family. Mark worked hard as he always felt a strong sense of duty to the bank and wanted to ensure that they were as efficient and as effective as possible. As the years stretched on, Mark found that he could no longer complete his working day between 8.30 am and 5 pm so he came to work earlier and left later each day. His 6 am start and 8 pm finish became normal and he also found that if he did a little bit of extra work at weekends, he could really get on top of things and the team were less stressed.

This work ethos continued for three years until one day at a usual team meeting Mark started to feel slightly dizzy and nauseous. He could hear bells ringing in his ear but tried to continue as normal. Once the meeting was over, he realised that no one had noticed and thought that maybe he was just unwell or had eaten something that disagreed with him over lunch. He thought nothing of it until the next day, when he was in the lift to his office and started to feel his heart thumping loudly in his chest and became really short of breath. He was with his colleague Rachel, who expressed concern and noticed how pale he had become. He admitted his symptoms and she prompted him to call the doctor. He reluctantly agreed and that afternoon found himself sitting across from the doctor explaining his symptoms. The doctor, who had seen this all before, explained that Mark was suffering from severe stress and needed to take some weeks off work in order to recover. Mark was utterly distraught and said that there was no possible way he could take any time off work as he simply didn't have any time. He left the doctor's feeling frightened and discussed the matter with his wife when he got home. She admitted that she too had noticed he was stressed and pleaded with him to listen to what the doctor had to say.

Mark took one month off work and started to realise that he had been forcing himself to work relentlessly and hadn't relaxed for a very long time. He realised that he had been extremely worried about losing his job and wanted to make sure the company could see that he was a dedicated employee. During his recovery time, he started to read about his symptoms and the impact of stress on the body. He undertook some physical activities such as yoga and meditation to help him relax.

He returned to work after a month but radically reduced his hours of work to normal working times and relished going home in the early evenings to spend time with his wife and family. The quality of his work actually improved and his team commented on how much easier he was to relate to as he was not in a permanent state of stress and anxiety. In fact, they commented that the office was a much calmer place. Mark is now recovered, but says that, almost like an alcoholic defaulting back to having a drink, he has tendencies to default into frenzied work activities, and has to be gently pulled back by colleagues or family to remind him of what has happened before. He is now very open about his experience and talks to his colleagues and younger members of the team to ensure that they know how to prevent similar situations.

Stories like Mark's are not uncommon in the corporate world where leaders give so much of themselves to their job with little emotional return. However, all of the emotions that they are experiencing or indeed repressing will eventually be released from their bodies and minds, usually in the most unhelpful way imaginable. If you are worried that you are stressed, here are some of the symptoms that you can look out for:

Symptoms of stress

▊ Feeling anxious, irritable or depressed.

▊ Apathy, loss of interest at work.

▊ Problems sleeping and subsequent fatigue.

▊ Muscle tension or headaches.

▊ Stomach problems.

▊ Social withdrawal.

▊ Abuse of food, alcohol or drugs.

Causes of stress

▊ Sometimes the stress you experience can be caused by an underlying emotion such as fear or anxiety of the unknown, losing your position or livelihood.

▊ It can also be driven by a real lack of understanding of your values and of where you are in your life and how you got there.

▊ You may have followed a well-worn path into your particular field of expertise but it bears no relation to what you are, in fact, passionate about.

▊ It is always worth taking some time to think about your life, what you are doing, why you are doing it and if there is an alternative that could make you happier and less stressed. I have met so many executives who could never imagine not doing their current role (no matter how utterly miserable they were), but when they were either forced to quit or decided to do so of their own accord, the transformation post change was utterly amazing. They have given themselves a happier and healthier (albeit sometimes poorer) existence and they feel utterly fulfilled.

▌ If you are not in a position to change your role, maintain your emotional health simply by integrating a small number of activities that will allow you both to process the emotions that have arisen during the day and consequently release them to free your physiology to refashion your mind for the following day at work.

Your emotional health plan

The mood meter (Figure 3.2) can help you to create a mood that is conducive to you being effective and indeed creative in your work. Some activities that can induce natural mood stimulation include the following:

▌ **Exercise.** Take regular exercise, preferably something that will raise your heart rate for 30 minutes each day. This can be something as simple as walking briskly, cycling, swimming or an exercise class in your lunch break. It takes great discipline to build this into your life but the effects on the body are hugely significant and pervasive. It will also offer a release after a busy or stressful day and reduce heart disease and risk of high blood pressure and stroke.

▌ **Food choices.** When you are stressed, the body works much harder to simply keep you functioning at a normal level. When the mind senses a threat (which, if you remember, manifests from an emotion or feeling), it injects flight or fight hormones into the body. These hormones pump a huge surge of energy into the bloodstream which is quickly followed by a natural crash of energy post-event. When you experience the crash, you crave to feel good again and do that by choosing sugary snacks, alcohol or foods with a high fat content which will bring you back to that wonderful high. This becomes a vicious cycle and a common feature of executives who are continuously on the go and keep reaching for easy food fixes in between meetings. It takes determination to break this cycle and there is now a world of food choices that can help you to become clean and balanced in your eating. It takes great willpower, but once you come off the treadmill of highs and lows from food, you will feel so much better physically and emotionally. There are thousands of food plans you can choose from. One that I have found particularly interesting is the *Deliciously Ella* cookbook (Yellow Kite Books, 2015), which is a plant-based vegan diet – following it takes discipline, but after a number of weeks you will notice a big change in your mood and energy.

▌**Sleep.** The topic of sleep is quite popular at the moment, as depicted by the findings of the Great British Sleep survey of 20,000 Britons, which found that poor sleep is widespread and is damaging quality of life. One of the sponsors of the sleep survey, Professor Russell Foster, Chair of Circadian Neuroscience and Head of the Sleep and Circadian Neuroscience Institute at the University of Oxford, said: 'Sleep is the single most important health behaviour we have. It affects everything from our day-to-day functioning to our long-term physical and mental health. We need to understand just how we're sleeping as a nation so we can start helping people sleep better and so lead healthier lives.' There are many sleep experts who can suggest a world of activities to help promote more restful sleep. Here is one example of some useful tips on how to improve sleep quality and quantity:

http://healthysleep.med.harvard.edu/healthy/getting/overcoming/tips

▌**Support.** Ironically, when you feel stressed you tend to isolate yourself even more which often deepens the problem. The effects of stress can cause people to retreat and, in fact, avoid other people as you simply don't have the energy to speak to people or pretend everything is OK. However, it is enormously important to have a support network, whether it is family or close colleagues at work, in whom you can confide. Usually, talking about things lessens the seriousness and can help bring perspective and some ideas on to how to lessen the stress. If you cannot confide in anyone, it may be worth thinking about eliciting the help of a professional, whether that is a qualified executive coach or a therapist who can help you work through the problems. There is very little stigma attached to this nowadays, and you might find that when you start to open up there are many people in your organisation who are going through similar situations and are only too eager to share their stories and experiences.

Your emotional resilience

All of the above tips can help you to manage your emotions in a way that is optimal for your mental and physical health. However, it is inevitable that sometimes you will be faced with periods where life-altering and earth-shattering events occur, such as a death or loss of a loved one. However, the human mind is well equipped to be able to deal with the most challenging of situations. Humans by their nature are extremely resilient beings. Think of those people who have historically experienced the worst atrocities known to mankind. They found some way to freeze the emotion for a period of time in order to get on with the business of surviving and hopefully living. The repressed emotion may have played havoc with their subsequent personal lives but they managed to rise from the ashes of whatever horror they encountered and put one foot in front of the other to continue with existing. Hopefully, the stresses that you are experiencing in the workplace are not as horrific, although sometimes they may feel that way, and there is a means for you to meet the emotion and investigate what is triggering such a visceral response in you. This type of emotional agility will endlessly help you to address these situations before they manifest as debilitating stress or breakdowns at work. Your resilience as a leader is key to ensuring that you can run a team or an organisation in a way that shows a good example and humility. You are not superhuman and, the more you try to maintain such a façade, the more difficult you make it for those around you to imitate such utterly unattainable traits. You will be far more effective as a leader if you are honest with those you trust about what is really going on for you and how you manage it.

The City Mental Health Alliance was set up in the UK by a group of senior executives to create an environment in the city of London where mental health was discussed in the same way as physical health. Their vision is to create a world where mental health is recognised as a boardroom issue and is essential to maximise business performance. They have quantified the cost of mental health illness to UK business as £26 billion.

> You will be far more effective as a leader if you are honest about what is really going on for you

EXERCISE 5.2

How to manage your emotions to reduce stress

- Describe the source of your stress at work. Is it a person who triggers your anxiety or fear of an event happening to you?

- Can you describe the pervading emotion inside of you as a result of this?

- What happens to your body, your mind? How do you sleep?

- What do you see as the worst thing that could happen to you? Describe it in vivid detail.

▍ Have you spoken to anyone about how you feel? If not, could you? And who could that be?

▍ How might they respond to you? Do you think it would help?

▍ Do you want this feeling to leave you?

▍ If so, what are the first steps you can take to start the process of feeling a little better?

IN SUMMARY

As we have discovered, it is indeed a wonderful skill to be able to assess, use and understand emotions, but you also need some strategies on how to manage the emotions that constantly arise in you as a leader. After reading this chapter:

▍ you will now be able to manage your emotional self effectively, which will help your leadership reputation as those leaders who demonstrate these qualities can usually instil increased followership and influence among their team and peers

▍ your new ability to manage emotions in yourself will reduce stress, increase resilience and help you remain balanced emotionally throughout challenging and ambiguous situations which you are faced with.

Step Six: managing emotions of others

Start with the end in mind

Stephen R. Covey,
*Seven Habits of Highly Effective People:
Powerful Lessons in Personal Change*

Get to know your team

As outlined in Step One of this book, you must get to know your team or peers in a way that is meaningful and not just transactional. To do this well, you need to spend time with each individual and collectively as a team. Only when you begin to build some meaningful relationships with those around you can you begin to assess people's motivational values. This will also help you gather valuable knowledge on their normal temperament so that you can spot any diversions away from this baseline. This takes time.

Let's plan how you might achieve this:

▌ How are you going to schedule the time to do this with the people in your team?

▌ What might prevent you?

▌ How will you overcome these barriers?

Spending time with staff is one of the most neglected areas of a leader's remit, as they believe that busyness, i.e. answering emails and attending every meeting they are invited to, is worthwhile for the organisation. Indeed, these activities are useful but only if they are selected carefully. In a self-assessment tool called Strengths Deployment Inventory (SDI), which helps people manage conflict and improve their relationships, there is a distinction between *rewarded* and *preferred* behaviour. In some organisations it becomes very clear very quickly that there is a way of working that is both prioritised and rewarded. The activities that it inspires may not remotely tie into the explicit metrics of the organisation but it is all that senior management refer to when they are looking for progress updates. Depending on the culture of the organisation and how it is led, there will often be a focus on what the CEO or head of division's interest is. As a leader it is worth examining what such rewarded behaviours are in your organisation so that you can then compare them with your preferred behaviours or way of working.

Spending long periods away from your values and comfort zone while in rewarded behaviour can not only be exhausting but might also cause you to neglect the needs of your team. Make some independent decisions as leader and subsequently prioritise your tasks in a way that will both develop your team to do their job well and allow you to think strategically about how to achieve an optimal organisational goal with the team or group of people that you have been tasked to manage. You can do this most efficiently by placing the right people in the right position, making sure that they are fully skilled and equipped to do the job without any hindrances, either emotional or otherwise.

Spending time with staff is one of the most neglected areas of a leader's remit

Benefits of knowing your team

In Step Two we talked about the Plutchik Wheel of Emotions which measured emotions from the least to the most intense. Your ability to spot the emotion at the least intense stage will in fact save you a lot of time later on as the person is still within rationality and you can possibly reason with them with some ease.

EXERCISE 6.1

How to manage emotions in others

Here, in no particular order, are some things to think about when you are managing emotions in others:

▌ There is a delicate balance between spotting the emotion and then deciding on how to manage it.

▌ If you have a good relationship with the person it will be much easier to work through as trust will have been established.

▌ It is not about tackling the person head-on but getting a deeper understanding of what the things are that are affecting them outside the particular incident which you are seeing them in.

▌ If you do spot some out-of-character behaviour, try to assess if something deeper is going on for the person. It is useful to:

  ▌ consider that this could be their preferred approach to everything, i.e. perhaps they are rather timid and often expect the worst to happen in any given situation

  ▌ try to manage any worries by asking them what is on their mind, listening carefully and, if possible, providing them with some assistance or support to help them progress.

How to change an emotional response in someone

When people are in an emotional state it is often difficult to reason with them, but there are a number of basic things you can do to begin to manage their emotional state. The examples that follow are, inevitably, quick sketches of some techniques to offer you some basic guidance that you can adjust to your own context, which indeed may be far more complex.

1. **Change their environment.** Often people (like the case study of Mark in Step Five) can become stressed at work, so removing them from the situation that is causing such anxiety can reduce any feelings of being threatened. This might simply be the suggestion of a walk outside or a coffee at the local coffee shop. It is important that you create a safe space so that they don't feel even more vulnerable and paranoid about the consequences of being taken away from their comfort zone. It might be good to ask them where they would like to go.

2. **Don't probe or be too pushy.** Some people need lots of time to be able to admit or even figure out what is going on for them. This might mean that you need to meet them more than once to get some idea of what might be happening. It is best to wait until they are ready as opposed to forcing them into admitting what is wrong.

3. **Ask questions and listen.** If someone is willing to open up to you, use some coaching and gentle probing techniques to start the process of understanding what is going on. This open space will give them time to reflect while answering and, hopefully, help to unravel what might be going on for them. Open questions such as What, Why, How, Tell me, are useful for eliciting a full answer using the person's own knowledge and feeling. It can be refreshing for people to be granted some time to talk through what might be going on for them. It is also important at this point to listen carefully with no distractions, such as a phone ringing or an imminent diary appointment with someone else straight after the meeting, which might cause you to be mentally absent from the discussion with this person.

4. **Don't judge.** As outlined in Step One of this book, we each live our lives by a different set of values. Therefore,

it is important that you don't impose your views too readily on the person who has chosen to open up to you. Their feelings are legitimate, and acknowledging that is a powerful step in ensuring that they will trust you enough to continue the conversation with you. It is possible that they are feeling a particular way because of other dimensions within their lives. However, by openly listening without judgement you can help them understand that what might be affecting them at work may be informed by a greater unresolved emotion.

5. **Get some help.** Most managers and leaders are relatively skilled in a lot of areas. However, if you do elicit some honest and thoughtful insight from those whose emotions you are trying to manage, always know how far to go in terms of your abilities as a psychologist or therapist. It is possible that some deep-rooted issue may arise, which is affecting the person's work, but you are not qualified or it is not safe for you to help them manage this to a conclusion. Most workplaces have counselling services or can refer such situations to qualified professionals who form part of the occupational health structure of the organisation. It is nice to do this in a way that is thoughtful and not dismissive, or makes the person feel like you have listened and are now shoving them off in a direction where your involvement ceases.

Managing the unmanageable

However, even when you diligently follow the above steps but continue to meet odd or unmanageable behaviours, it may be that the other individual has absolutely no idea what is actually going on for them. This can be more dangerous than anything else, as the person can cause maximum destruction to those around them and utterly convince themselves that they are completely right and everyone else is wrong. The reality is that this is entirely fantasy-led and a dangerous journey to go on with someone.

CASE STUDY

The dark side of emotional agility

Here is an example of a manager who met someone who had deep-seated emotional and, indeed, psychological problems, but no amount of work could help her recognise, or indeed manage, her problems.

Matt hired Carly for a senior role in his large professional services firm. He was quite surprised to read her CV as she had previously worked for firms that were much larger and more reputable than his firm. He was pleased when she arrived for interview and was really impressed by her humility and willingness to come and work for a smaller company so that she could really make a difference to those around her in the new organisation.

Matt knew that hiring Carly would require a very different set of leadership skills from those required for the rest of his team, as Carly was very experienced and wouldn't take too kindly to being closely managed or made accountable for her work. Matt decided to take the chance and make the most of this talent, which he felt fortunate that the company had stumbled upon. Within a few weeks, Matt started to hear some comments from his colleagues that Carly was quite difficult and rather abrasive. He held off on judgement as he knew that she was just finding her feet and decided that that was probably distracting her from this new role. He continued to work on the relationship and gave Carly lots of time to regularly offload her thoughts and experiences with him. She sometimes inferred that her colleagues were inferior in intellect, which made Matt uncomfortable, but he listened and encouraged her to work with others and really get to know the organisation. He noticed that sometimes Carly tended to have quite a distorted view of reality – a very different version of the realities painted by her colleagues.

After a period of six months in the job and a series of weekly meetings, Matt decided that he would need to reduce their meetings to every two to three weeks so that he could reduce the dependency on him and hopefully Carly could start to trust others around him. Unknown to him, Carly was furious. She took it as an enormous insult and started to become paranoid that Matt was plotting to remove her from the organisation. Matt was indeed oblivious to this paranoia as Carly never expressly communicated how their reduced contact made her feel. Instead of keeping in touch with her, Matt hoped the vacuum that he had created by reducing their meetings would encourage her to seek out other colleagues and begin to build relationships. This turned out to be a major mistake on his part.

A number of weeks later, when Matt enquired of his colleagues how Carly was doing, one suggested that she was feeling very left out of the team. Matt immediately reached out to Carly to meet for coffee and a chat and she agreed to meet with him a few days later. When Carly arrived at the meeting, Matt could see that her body language was really closed and she was angry. Matt asked her how she was doing and she erupted furiously and accused him of undermining her and not giving her the same chances as everyone else at the firm. Matt was astonished. He had, in fact, worked hard to ensure that Carly was well placed on special projects and was ready to place her on a forthcoming highly prestigious project. Matt tried to reason with her but she was angry, stating that Matt was incompetent and everyone in the organisation thought so, too. Matt decided to bring the meeting to a close and suggested that they could perhaps meet at a later date. Carly stormed out of the room. A number of days later, Carly went to Matt's boss and threatened to make a formal complaint about him, suggesting that he had behaved badly towards her by taking some projects from her and was inhibiting her from progressing through the organisation. Matt was shocked and felt betrayed after investing so much time in Carly and defending her to those who were highly sceptical of her.

This case study illustrates the high level of complexity that exists within those around us. You may do your very best to manage and lead people, but the realities of the rather overloaded minds of people often result in situations such as that described, leaving you, as a leader, a vulnerable target to people like Carly.

It turns out that Carly had deep psychological issues that she had learnt to hide and had become quite the expert at presenting herself as a charming genius who was excellent at her job. The reality was very different. She had become skilled at disguising her anxiety through admonishing others and continuously criticising those around her as if they were the cause of all the things that were going wrong in the world. She built her own reality, which involved zero self-awareness on her side, as she had established enough power and credibility to undermine any person who dared to question her loyalty or dedication. When anyone tried to get beneath the surface of what was really going on, she found a way to twist the conversation back towards the person and accused them of harassing her – the ultimate scare tactic, which is abused by so many like Carly in the workplace, often by people who manifest with psychopathic tendencies. It is useful as a leader to know what these tendencies look like and how to manage them,

Psychopathy at work

There have been some books written on the fact that a lot of organisations are indeed harbouring psychopaths. In Babiak and Hare's book *Snakes in Suits* (2006), they suggest that one in every hundred members of the population meet the psychopathic scale and the proportion could be as high as one in ten senior executives in the workplace. Traits such as ruthlessness, fearlessness, charm, persuasiveness, egocentricity, impulsiveness and the absence of conscience and empathy are common personality traits. Here are some of the common traits of a psychopath at work:

▌ **Emotional manipulators.** Poor performers with psychopathic tendencies may frequently appeal to extenuating circumstances and make pleas for support and understanding in order to shift the focus from their own behaviour. This can be very difficult for you as a leader to get a handle on, as, for example, in Carly's case, her behaviour was most likely a pre-emptive strike to disguise the fact that she was not going to make her targets for the year.

▌ **Charm offensive.** Psychopaths at work are masters at making brilliant first impressions and can come across as very charming. They turn on the charm quite early in the relationship and then reduce it slowly to engender some doubt in the person they are manipulating. They often sweep people off their feet, making them feel like they are the only person in the room, but the residual feeling from the victim may be one of confusion and insecurity after the event.

▌ **Narcissistic.** Most psychopaths are completely self-interested and have an arrogant, grandiose and egocentric interpersonal style. Relationship patterns in both their personal and corporate lives are often stormy and short-lived. They also see themselves as more skilled then others around them and spend a lot of time waiting for such accolades, hence the scale of Carly's reaction in Matt's office.

▌ **Nothing sticks.** Psychopaths never accept responsibility for their mistakes and poor behaviour. They are also excellent at manufacturing evidence, which can make others look guilty, so that they can quickly shift the blame from themselves.

▌ **No emotions.** For most psychopaths the part of the brain responsible for emotion is turned down (or even off), meaning that he or she doesn't experience normal feelings like the rest of society. They are unfamiliar with fear, regret, disgust and shame. They are excellent at acting out emotions such as being scared, sorry or surprised in order to manipulate others if it will help them advance their own agenda. If you have a colleague who is prone to extreme displays of emotion then quickly returns to normal as if nothing has happened, then you might question whether he or she really feels anything at all.

The above list can help you recognise people who have psychopathic tendencies – however, it is important that you don't treat everyone who displays a lack of empathy or acts in an arrogant way as a psychopath.

How to deal with a psychopath at work

It is useful to understand what these people might look like in reality. Dr John Clarke offers some advice on how to deal with such individuals:

1. Educate yourself about psychopaths: it is useful to know what you are dealing with.

2. Don't get isolated. It is most likely that other people are suffering as well.

3. Get support, talk to family and friends. If things heighten, talk to your manager or the human resource department.

4. Promote yourself in the company, let other people know early on of your achievements before the office psychopath steals them or tries to destroy your reputation.

5. Remove psychopaths from the organisation as fast as you possibly can. It may sound defeatist but an exit strategy can be the best approach for such unmanageable people.

You will be glad to read that managing emotions in more stable people is a little easier. Hopefully, you will be able to spot the behaviours early enough to try to make a difference and intercept them before they become damaging to the person or the organisation.

EXERCISE 6.2

Understanding an extreme emotional response

Think of a situation in which one of your team responded with a high level of emotion that seemed disproportionate to the event that triggered it.

▍ Describe the situation, the context, the other people involved.

▍ What was the overt emotion displayed by the team member?

▍ What effect did it have on those around them? What did they do or say?

▍ Thinking about the person, what is their usual or prevailing mood?

▍ Did you take some time to understand what might have been going on for them?

▍ Did you get to the bottom of what was going on for them that evoked such a response?

▍ What have you learnt about the person as a result?

IN SUMMARY

Recognising and managing emotions in yourself is one challenge but one of the most difficult tasks as a leader is the management of emotions in others. You will see from reading this chapter that, in developing such a skill, you need to consider what can be unpredictable behaviours and reactions from those whom you are trying to manage. A direct approach that might involve you walking up to individuals and offering an uninvited diagnosis is often highly contentious. Alternatively, you cannot hope that whatever issues someone is going through will be resolved by studiously ignoring the problem.

Therefore, taking the time to recognise the emotion, following it, understanding what might be behind it can start the process of moving people from one mood to another. It takes real skill and patience, neither of which can be learned overnight, but once you have mastered them, it will help you feel more confident when facing difficult interactions and also enable you to build deeper and stronger connections with those around you.

Step Seven: creating awareness

Knowing yourself is the beginning of all wisdom.

Aristotle

Take some time

As you can see from the previous six steps, becoming emotionally agile takes time, energy and interest in order to get to know yourself and your teams. One of the most challenging aspects for most leaders we meet is understanding how important it is to take the time to reflect and get to know yourself and those around you. Often, leaders are rewarded for doing task-oriented aspects and not these emotionally intelligent aspects of leadership. Kotter's work on the difference between leadership and management (see Kotter, 2001) talks about management being about convergence and leadership being about divergence. Most contemporary organisations reward activities in the convergence spectrum because they are visible and immediate. Building relationships and being emotionally agile is on the divergence spectrum – discontinuous innovation, doing different things, generating change through people and so on. It is valued in the abstract but rarely rewarded in the concrete. It is worth assessing which of these approaches your organisation rewards. For the purpose of increasing your emotional agility, let's now work on the latter.

EXERCISE 7.1

Scheduling time to think

▌ When was the last time you completely cleared your diary for one hour, not checking your emails, going to meetings or engaging with others?

▌ If not, why not? How useful would you consider an exercise like this?

▌ Set aside an hour in your schedule to spend time reflecting on how things are going for you in general. It may be useful to note down some ideas on paper.

Here are some possible questions to think about:

▌ What is making you happy at work?

▌ What is keeping you awake at night?

▌ What have you learnt about yourself in the last three months?

▌ Who are you now? Use some adjectives to describe yourself.

▌ What would you like to have more of in your life?

▌ What are the two steps you can take to bring more reflection into your life?

All of these questions may seem entirely unrelated to business or successfully achieving your work goals. However, training your mind to recognise the impact of your own behaviour, both on your work and on those around you, is a useful skill to learn early on in your career.

When asked to reflect back on the most important aspect of their careers, most of the senior leaders we meet wish they had spent more time reflecting on what really made them happy when they were young leaders. In their frenzy of ambition and fear of losing position on their career path, some had ceased to reflect on who they really were as individuals. The 'World Happiness Report' of 2015 (Helliwell, Layard and Sachs, 2015) reveals that, 'Life satisfaction depends on strong social support networks, on generosity and voluntarism, on "generalized trust" among strangers in the society, and on the trust in government'. The report suggests that, in order to improve happiness in society, education, including moral education and mindfulness training or reflection, plays an important role. To help you reflect on whether you are satisfied in your life, here are some methods that can help you start the journey of reflection and self-awareness.

How to become self-aware

If you are uncertain or unsuited to taking time out to reflect, there are a number of things that you can do to encourage such behaviour.

Reflection through action research

Action learning is described as taking the time to consider alternatives and make comparisons. This is a skill set that is learned over time and is one of the most powerful skills a leader can have. We work with executives using an *action learning* process that is linked to whatever process of change participants might be experiencing. The process offers them time to think and reflect on the organisational changes or situations they are engaged in. Whilst in the process of implementing these changes, they reflect on and modify their practice. As a research methodology, it combines action and systematic reflection to address a question. It has dual aims: to know more about the issues being studied (a research aim) and to try to change it (an action aim). In this respect, *action learning* is a process where participants make sense of and theorise about their own work. It is highly practical, but because the analysis is embedded in the particularities of the context, it is immediately applicable. Therefore, the next time you find yourself in a situation that feels complex or unmanageable, identify a peer or mentor with whom you can discuss the issue to gain an understanding of what is happening to you. You can then work through the steps of finding your emotional agility to assess how you or the other person might be feeling. Then take the time to understand the issue and try to manage any emotions in yourself and others.

> Action learning is taking the time to consider alternatives and make comparisons

Mindfulness

The concept of mindfulness, which has its origins in Buddhist traditions, has been popularised in the last few years and has underpinned well-being strategies for leaders in business, schools, prisons and government departments. Mindfulness describes and advocates *quality of attention,* which is dependent upon and influenced by the nature of our thoughts, speech and actions. It offers us a way to become wiser in our actions and introduce more social harmony and compassion to those around us. It has also been met with some scepticism so it is good to reflect on how it has evolved and if it might be, in your view, a legitimate means of generating self-awareness.

Opinion: mindfulness in business – real or a ploy?

Mindfulness has become a popular topic across the business media, featuring, for example, in an article in the *Financial Times* newspaper in May 2014 (Agnew). This describes mindfulness as 'the latest popular movement in mental wellbeing' and discusses the quiet revolution that is gripping the City of London. Large financial houses, such as KPMG, Goldman Sachs, Unilever and the Bank of England have presented mindfulness in well-being seminars and encourage staff to use meditation apps such as Headspace. It has become an adopted stress-relief technique for some finance professionals and aims to encourage greater clarity of thought in a world dominated by technology. The concept is gaining traction as a legitimate way to reduce stress and offer health benefits.

Mindfulness is now a mainstream topic within leadership programmes in many business schools – Ashridge Business School and Cranfield Business School have an open programme dedicated to the subject, while IMD, Harvard, Claremont and Drucker School are just a few others who reference mindfulness in their programmes.

However, a cynical or alternative view could suggest that companies are using concepts such as mindfulness to avoid the ultimate responsibility for burdening employees with stress in the first place. Offering courses in mindfulness may just shift the burden onto the individual employee, framing stress as a personal problem with mindfulness as the antidote to help employees continue to work within fundamentally toxic environments. The manifesto of offering mindfulness, often cloaked in an aura of care and humanity, may give employees a means to cope with the stresses and strains of corporate life, but doesn't address the architects of such stress. It must be the organisation's responsibility to abstain from sending their employees into severe states of stress through sheer apathy, neglect or on purpose.

Benefits of mindfulness

Ploy or not, Davis and Hayes (2012) in the *American Psychological Association Journal* suggest that mindfulness meditation promotes meta-cognitive awareness and enhances attentional capacities through gains in working memory.

They suggest that such cognitive gains, in turn, contribute to effective emotion-regulation strategies. They identified a number of key benefits:

▌**Reduced rumination.** Several studies have shown that mindfulness reduces rumination. In one study, for example, Chambers *et al.* (2008) asked twenty novice meditators to participate in a ten-day intensive mindfulness meditation retreat. After the retreat, the meditation group had significantly higher self-reported mindfulness, and experienced fewer depressive symptoms and less rumination. The study also demonstrated that meditators had significantly better working memory capacity and were better able to sustain attention during a performance task compared with the control group.

▌**Stress reduction.** Many studies show that practising mindfulness reduces stress. In 2010, Hoffman *et al.* conducted a meta-analysis of 39 studies that explored the use of mindfulness-based stress reduction and mindfulness-based cognitive therapy. The findings offer evidence that mindfulness meditation increases positive affect and decreases anxiety and negative affect. The researchers also separately found that the participants who experienced mindfulness-based stress reduction had significantly less anxiety, depression and somatic distress compared with the control group.

▌**Boosts to working memory.** Improvements to working memory appear to be another benefit of mindfulness, research finds. A 2010 study by Jha *et al.*, for example, documented the benefits of mindfulness meditation among a military group who participated in an eight-week mindfulness training, a non-meditating military group and a group of non-meditating civilians. Both military groups were in a highly stressful period before deployment. The researchers found that the non-meditating military group had decreased working memory capacity over time, whereas working memory capacity among non-meditating civilians was stable across time. Within the meditating military group, however, working memory capacity increased with meditation practice. In addition, meditation practice was directly related to self-reported positive affect and inversely related to self-reported negative affect.

▍**Focus.** Another study examined how mindfulness meditation affected participants' ability to focus attention and suppress distracting information. The researchers compared a group of experienced mindfulness meditators with a control group that had no meditation experience. They found that the meditation group had significantly better performance on all measures of attention and had higher self-reported mindfulness. Mindfulness meditation practice and self-reported mindfulness were correlated directly with cognitive flexibility and attentional functioning (Moore and Malinowski, 2009).

▍**Less emotional reactivity.** Research also supports the notion that mindfulness meditation decreases emotional reactivity. In a study of people who had anywhere from one month to twenty-six years of mindfulness meditation practice, researchers found that mindfulness meditation practice helped people disengage from emotionally upsetting pictures and enabled them to focus better on a cognitive task compared with people who saw the pictures but did not meditate (Ortner *et al.*, 2007).

▍**More cognitive flexibility.** Another line of research suggests that in addition to helping people become less reactive, mindfulness meditation may also give them greater cognitive flexibility. One study found that people who practise mindfulness meditation appear to develop the skill of self-observation, which neurologically disengages the automatic neural pathways (described earlier) that were created by prior learning and enables present-moment input to be integrated in a new way (Siegel, 2007). Meditation also activates the brain region associated with more adaptive responses to stressful or negative situations (Cahn and Polich, 2006; Davidson *et al.*, 2003).

▌ **Relationship satisfaction.** Several studies find that a person's ability to be mindful can help predict relationship satisfaction – the ability to respond well to relationship stress and the skill in communicating one's emotions to a partner. Empirical evidence suggests that mindfulness protects against the emotionally stressful effects of relationship conflict (Barnes *et al.*, 2007), is positively associated with the ability to express oneself in various social situations (Dekeyser *et al.*, 2008) and predicts relationship satisfaction (Barnes *et al.*, 2007; Wachs and Cordova, 2007).

▌ **Other benefits.** Mindfulness has been shown to enhance self-insight, morality, intuition and fear modulation, all functions associated with the brain's middle prefrontal lobe area. Evidence also suggests that mindfulness meditation has numerous health benefits, including increased immune functioning (Davidson *et al.*, 2003; see Grossman, Niemann, Schmidt and Walach, 2004 for a review of physical health benefits), improvement to well-being (Carmody and Baer, 2008) and reduction in psychological distress (Coffey and Hartman, 2008; Ostafin *et al.*, 2006). In addition, mindfulness meditation practice appears to increase information processing speed (Moore and Malinowski, 2009), as well as decrease task effort and thoughts that are unrelated to the task at hand (Lutz *et al.*, 2009).

EXERCISE 7.2

How to practise mindfulness

If mindfulness is something that you find appealing as a means to begin to increase your self-awareness and emotional agility, then there are a number of helpful tips that can help you to begin to explore how you might practise mindfulness (courtesy of *Mindful* magazine 2014).

Location

It's best to find a spot at home that is free from clutter and noise. If there is no natural light available you can leave the lights on. Outside locations are also fine, as long as they offer peace and quiet.

Posture

Find a comfortable position to sit. *Mindful* magazine shows you how to organise your posture.

FIGURE 7.1 Mindfulness posture

Time

Set aside some practice time. It is good to decide on a specific amount of time at the start so you are not worrying about when to stop. If you are just starting out, five to ten minutes is ideal. As you progress with your practice, you can slowly build up to forty-five minutes or an hour. Most people meditate either first thing in the morning or later in the evening (or both). If your lifestyle is too busy to allow for these sorts of regular sessions, do not worry if you can't always fit it in. Remember that doing something is better than doing nothing.

Breathing

Once you are happy with your posture, begin to follow your breath as it goes in and out. Before long, you will find your attention wandering from your breath to other places. If you come round to noticing this after a few minutes or seconds, simply return your attention back to the flow of your breathing. Don't worry about thinking certain thoughts (or not) or try to force your mind down specific routes. Your attention will wander and then return. Just because it's a simple thing to do, it doesn't mean it's also easy. It is worth remembering that Buddhist monks have spent thousands of years perfecting the art of true meditation, and the modern concept of mindfulness offers a tiny but helpful introduction to help you pause and focus your unwieldy mind and channel your breath to find some space and step out of your busy world for a short time.

Practice

No different to training for a marathon or playing the violin, the best way to become good at mindfulness is to be diligent about your practice and build it into your routine. Continuance will help you build up a repository of calm in your body and mind which will help you when you do encounter the roadblocks along the way.

Mindfulness and emotional agility

All the principles outlined in Part 1 of this book on how to recognise, understand and manage emotions in yourself and others can be a difficult ask if you are continuously swept up in the frenzy of your life. Most people who are good at emotional agility are keen observers of human behaviour and always take the time to pay close attention to the actions and words that exist behind the behaviours. These people are not necessarily born in this way but have consciously gained some skill or have had an emotional jolt that has forced them to confront their place in the world and spend some time immersed in a deep feeling of some sort. This has helped them rebalance their view on the world and approach life with a degree of measure and less fear. Perhaps the worst thing has already happened to them, so they no longer run through life with fear driving their ambitions or activities. Perhaps they have also experienced many stages of emotions and recognise the intensity and overt behaviours that accompany such states. They now may be more attuned to their own feelings and really understand how to manage them and channel them into something useful or use the strategies to change them if and when appropriate.

This is not to say that you need to go through a life-altering experience in order to become emotionally agile, but if you consciously wish to improve that aspect of your perspective then, like running a marathon, you have to start training slowly in order to prepare your body for an effort it may not be accustomed to. Using action learning and practising mindfulness offers a means to reflect on how you work as a leader. It will help you to take some time to step back and consider how you are feeling and why and help you make more measured decisions as to how you can cope in a way that is less strenuous.

IN SUMMARY

You should now have obtained some insight into how you can manage yourself and your emotions through a combination of reflection and practising mindfulness. There are many methods to help you step back and reflect on who you are, helping you to explore what you are doing and why. These philosophical questions may seem unrelated to business but in reality are hugely important to your effectiveness as an emotionally agile leader. The next section will explore how you put all of these new skills into action for all the practical tasks you face as a leader.

2

Emotional agility in action

This part offers the reader some context in which to apply each or some of the seven steps outlined in Part 1. A number of typical activities will be examined that will take you though some real-life case studies within a variety of business contexts. These activities include: difficult performance appraisal conversations, motivating a disengaged team, increasing creativity and innovation in your organisation and, finally, how to become a more influential leader using your skills in EA. Such activities are often a key part of a leader's role and the book examines how emotional agility can help to overcome some of these challenges and offer improved followership as well as less stress for the leader involved.

Using EA for difficult performance appraisals

This chapter offers some suggestions on how to use all of the EA processes to help you prepare and deliver specific feedback to increase performance without damaging the relationship with your team.

Purpose of performance appraisals

Performance appraisals are a method of evaluating and assessing the job performance of an employee through the use of measures such as quality, quantity, cost and time. In general, performance appraisals are used to:

■ give feedback on performance to employees

■ identify employee training needs

■ document criteria used to allocate organisational rewards

■ form a basis for personnel decisions: salary increases, promotions, disciplinary actions, etc.

Performance appraisals are usually scheduled once a year, which is a useful marker in the diary for managers and their subordinates to get together. However, feedback organisations that offer consistent and regular feedback throughout the year are among the most successful as there is a continuous awareness generated around areas of good and poor performance. An organisational culture that readily prompts and invites all sorts of feedback, in particular immediately after events have taken place, is a feature of highly self-aware organisations continuously looking to improve performance across the board. There is something very brave about a culture where people are honest with each other when things go wrong and, conversely, are able to offer positive affirmations when things go well. A lot of organisations avoid the culture of feedback and tend to wait until the end of year review to collate and administer all feedback, good and bad, which can be utterly overwhelming for the recipient. The reason for this is that the focus is usually on the negative feedback, which overshadows what they did well. Perceived negative feedback is often taken very badly, as most people strive to be liked and admired for what they do.

Some Fortune 500 companies, such as General Electric (GE), are now looking at ways to depart from formal annual appraisals towards an assessment model throughout the year. Using mobile phone software, they encourage all employees to document good behaviour or that which adheres to the values of GE; this is captured and subsequently collated by the appropriate line manager, who offers this feedback at various stages throughout the year. This method has proved to be far more effective in promoting good behaviour in their organisation, encouraging a feedback culture and also prompting others to follow suit to act out the GE values. A win–win situation.

Conducting performance appraisals is one of the basic functions within a line management role. They are often viewed as a rather tedious administrative exercise that bears little relation to how real performance is measured. Some managers will instinctively know well in advance of a performance appraisal how someone in their team is doing. That is because their measure of a good employee or team member is often beyond what is outlined in the appraisal metrics. Reputation is everything and, if you have had a team member who has spent the year working really hard, being productive, inclusive and demonstrates willingness to work on tasks outside their remit, most line managers comfortably assess the person without ever having a formal appraisal. However, performance appraisals exist for good reason, often to help those who have potential for promotion so that all the formal metrics and qualitative information are in place to support the application. Conversely, if someone is performing poorly, it is helpful to sit down and assess where the areas for improvement are so that you can jointly work out a plan on how to get there.

> Most line managers should be able to comfortably assess their staff outside of a formal appraisal

CASE STUDY

Performance appraisal in action

It's time for James's performance appraisal. Dave, who is James's boss, has twelve appraisals to get through and is not really looking forward to conducting them. He has scheduled one hour for each appraisal, which he thinks should be plenty of time. It is always such a chore filling out the paperwork and having to think of nice things to say about each member of his team. Dave mostly likes to focus on areas for improvement as he thinks that the only way the organisation is going to progress is if people really focus on how to get better at their job. He acknowledges that it is a good chance to catch up with each member of the team and find out how things are going for them. They don't really share that much of a personal nature with him and he is not sure why that is the case. Perhaps it is better that they all keep a professional distance so that they can get on with their job. He puts together a list of improvements for each member of the team and notices how irritated he feels about how much needs to be improved to get the team back on track. A knock comes on the door. His first 'victim', James, arrives in his office. He remembers that James did quite a good job on a project a number of months ago and writes a note to remind himself to tell James that he was happy with this work.

James slowly makes his way towards his boss's office. It's his performance appraisal and he is absolutely dreading it. It's the same every year: long uncomfortable silences while his boss Dave goes through the appraisal form in great detail, sighing loudly and noting how James has self-scored his performance and usually suggesting changing it to reflect a lower score. James thinks that it is some psychological plan of Dave's to make him work harder. It actually has the opposite effect. It serves to make James feel worse, with no motivation, and leaves him wondering why he bothers putting in any effort in the first place. It's also unclear what it is that Dave wants James to achieve for the year. It is so unclear that James feels rather foolish asking his boss what his exact targets are, so he doesn't say anything and hopes he will work it out for himself. It's also the only time of the year that Dave has any interaction with James and tries to be friendly. It's embarrassing. The conversation is usually one-way with Dave doing all the talking and James just nodding apathetically in pseudo agreement. James leaves the meeting feeling worse and is now definitely determined to update his profile on jobs.com to find someone better to work for. That improves his mood...

This case study is a good example of how most performance appraisals go. They are formal meetings, and it can be very hard to really get to grips with what is going on with your staff if these appraisals are the only time when you meet with them to discuss how things are going. The example above demonstrates poor emotional agility on Dave's part as he is so busy being rational and ticking the boxes he has not bothered to see how James is feeling about things. If Dave invested some time building relationships and exploring what is happening for James, he would notice that such knowledge is a powerful mechanism to unlock better performance and a more motivated workforce. It may seem like a lot of time to invest in someone, but the returns are enormous.

How do we measure real performance?

A common approach to assessing performance is to use a numerical or scalar rating system whereby managers are asked to score an individual against a number of objectives/attributes. In some companies, employees receive assessments from their manager, peers, subordinates and customers while also performing a self-assessment. This is known as 360° appraisal.

Most organisations will have good appraisal frameworks to assess the quality of the work of their employees. An example of a traditional nine-box grid, which assesses potential and performance, is outlined below.

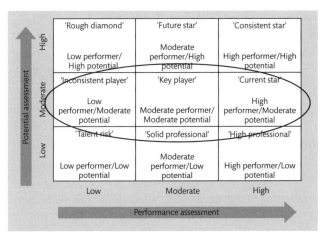

FIGURE 8.1 Nine-box grid

Source: Karen N. Caruso, http://web.viapeople.com/viaPeople-blog/bid/82257/Developing-Future-Promise-Use-the-9-Box-to-Develop-Talent-in-Succession-Planning

If you have worked hard to provide as much support as possible and that person is still operating in the bottom left-hand side of the grid, it is perhaps time to offer some feedback on their actual performance, and commence a performance improvement plan (PIP) or an exit plan for the said employee. For some managers these conversations can be easily done and they give them little thought. For others it can be an extremely painful process both for the manager and the employee. However, this definitely does not need to be the case.

The steps to less painful appraisals

1 Preparation is key

It is very useful to be well prepared in advance of your performance appraisal meetings. The reason for this, as we explained earlier, is that it is important to understand how each of your team or reports will respond in any given situation. Spending some time assessing how each person has done on paper in relation to the metrics that you have set out clearly at the beginning of the appraisal year will help you quantitatively assess how your team member has performed. One of the most common causes of difficulties in team members failing to reach their targets is a lack of clear target guidelines set out at the beginning of the appraisal year.

> Team members often fail to reach their targets due to a lack of clear guidelines at the beginning of the year

EXERCISE 8.1

Setting clear and achievable goals for your team

Now think about your team.

▌ Do you know exactly what each member is supposed to achieve for the year ahead?

▌ Have you communicated this clearly both verbally and in writing and received a confirmed response to such an instruction?

▌ Who are the individuals you are most concerned about in terms of achieving their targets? Why is this the case?

▌ What are the steps you will need to take during the year to ensure these individuals get the support they need?

▌ Are they aware that they are possibly off target? How often have you met with them to find out what is going on for them beyond their performance deficiencies?

As you can see from this exercise, poor performance is often as much the responsibility of you as the leader as it is of the individual themselves. A lot of poor-performing team members do not begin their professional lives aspiring to be poor performers but often end up in such scenarios due to weak instruction and little or no understanding of the context in which they are working. There is a huge responsibility on you as their manager to ensure that you create the environment in which they can work productively and achieve their targets. Most individuals do not want the stigma of being poor performers and, once they earn that title, it can end up as a downward spiral as they don't feel they can shake off the image that has been created.

2 Useful feedback models to help you appraise

There are a number of models that can help you during the appraisal period. These help to encapsulate many aspects of emotional agility as they tap into how the person is feeling and how you can use that to help them improve performance. We will examine two in particular: the BOFF model (behaviour, outcome, feeling and future) and the Coaching Feedback model (**www.performancetrainingorganisation.com**).

▌**The BOFF (behaviour, outcome, feeling and future) model**
offers a means to communicate the goal of the feedback to
the assessed in order to raise awareness of their behaviour,
and to understand its effect on others and what response
it provokes from others. The model allows you to learn to
see yourself as other people do. This encourages emotional
agility as you need to step out of the behaviour and assess
its impact on those around you. The BOFF model is very
easy to use.

For example:

Behaviour: describe the behaviour: 'You are sometimes
late sending the end of month report to me.'

Outcome: explain what impact that behaviour had on you:
'Because of this lateness, I cannot complete the divisional
report and submit to the board on time.'

Feelings: describe how this made you feel: 'It irritates me to
have to chase you for it and the board become annoyed with
me for delaying the overall reporting data for the month.'

In the last step of the feedback you must draw up your future
expectation, which includes the solution of the problem.

Future: 'Please can you try to compile and send the
report to me earlier, so that we can begin to regain our
reputation with the board as a professional division
that is organised and efficient?'

We work extensively with managers who have used the
BOFF with great success. It takes time and practice but is a
brilliant way of using your emotional agility skills to offer
feedback in a way that is practical and also understandable
for the recipient.

▌**The Coaching Feedback model** involves asking people to
give themselves the feedback instead of, or before, giving
yours. The model is based on the framework of traditional
coaching model GROW, developed by Sir John Whitmore,
which examines goal, reality, options and will. The best way

to think of its application is if you plan a journey, you first decide where you are going (the goal), and then establish where you currently are (your current reality). You then explore various routes (the options) to your destination. In the final step, establishing the will, you ensure that you're committed to making the journey, and are prepared for the obstacles that you might meet on the way.

The Coaching Feedback model builds on this and the authors advocate asking a number of questions that help prompt such self-reflective feedback in order to develop your staff:

1. What did you notice about your performance?
2. What do you like about what you did?
3. What I liked was...
4. If you could do it again, what would you do differently?
5. What will it be like when you can do that?
6. Can I make a suggestion?
7. What will you do about it in the future?

You will notice that these questions are open in nature, which means that the individual focuses on the positives and hopefully will also notice what didn't go so well. This is far more effective than approaching the appraisal with a list of all the things they did badly, as they will have had no time to reflect themselves on their progress or failures. It has been demonstrated from Step Three of this book that not displaying sensitivity or empathy in communication, especially during hierarchical exchanges (between a manager and a subordinate), can often unintentionally trigger dormant emotions in others which causes a subsequent hijack, reducing their ability to process any of what you have just said.

Using the Coaching Feedback model in the case study mentioned at the beginning of this chapter would allow

Dave to really get to know what are James's values, and how he thinks about and subsequently rates himself. It will also prompt James to reflect and think about what he could do better. This is far more powerful than Dave suggesting it, as he hasn't earned James's trust or respect to do so. It would also give Dave a chance to get to know James and his baseline expression and emotions so that he can subtly assess any deviation away from these.

Let's prepare for your next appraisal meeting

Think of the next appraisal you have scheduled with a member of your team. How can you now prepare and conduct the meeting in a way that is effective for you, the team member and the organisation? Here are a number of key steps to help you:

1. **Prepare for the meeting.** Gather together all the relevant data and some feedback from peers and other members of the organisation.

2. **First focus on the individual and assess their mood prior to commencing the feedback.** Are they stressed or worried? What effect will this have on their ability to listen?

3. **What mood are you in?** Have you cleared your mind and focused on the task at hand? This will help you to ensure that the appraisee meets a person who is open and ready to listen.

4. **Try to schedule enough time for the appraisal** so you have time to relax initially and find out how the person is getting on prior to launching into the formalities.

5. **Invest some time in the person prior to the meeting.** Ensure that you have had a number of interactions with them so that you can at least start to build a relationship that will induce trust and mutual respect. It will also

help you find out what is important to the person so you can shape a development plan to suit this.

6. **Ensure your meeting space is conducive to a positive outcome.** Avoid sitting behind a desk and try to arrange the seats so you are seated alongside each other.

7. **Ensure there are no interruptions.** Under no circumstances entertain any interruptions, including phone calls or emergency call-outs from your secretary or team. This shows a serious lack of respect for the other person.

8. **Use the feedback models outlined** and try to work with the person as opposed to working against them. If there are difficult messages to communicate, ensure you deliver them in a way that is not demeaning or destructive. This will possibly prompt the appraisee to shut down and the message will be lost anyway.

9. **Practise, practise.** Appraisals get easier with time. They are even enjoyable when you have built enough of a relationship with your team so that you all enjoy getting together to discuss performance successes and failures.

10. **Use the opportunity of appraisals** to really gain an understanding of how each individual in your team could contribute to something worthwhile and innovative for the department. Think beyond the meeting to what you can create with the collective abilities you have.

IN SUMMARY

Appraisals can be either painful or productive processes. A little preparation will really help you to avoid awkward situations that are damaging both to your relationship with the employee and their own psychological contract with the organisation. You should now be able to conduct your assessment of your team in a way that is emotionally agile and productive for you both by following a few easy steps.

9

How to motivate a disengaged team using EA

This chapter focuses on how you can first spot a disengaged team and, second, use the emotional agility skills you have learnt to try to get the team back on track. It will also offer some suggestions about how using EA can help diagnose the barriers of team motivation, remove them and build a sustainable high-performing culture.

EXERCISE 9.1

Assessing your team

▌ What size team do you currently have?

▌ Can you name each of the team members and list what you think possibly motivates each?

▌ Where are they located? Locally or internationally?

▌ Who are the star players, medium performers and poor performers?

▌ What has the team performance been like over the past (a) month, (b) six months, (c) year?

▌ Have there been any changes in context or to the members of the team?

▌ Are your team all very similar in personality and style or completely different?

▎ What are your expectations of the team? Are these expectations met (a) regularly, (b) sometimes, (c) never?

▎ If (c) never, why do you think this is the case?

▎ Have you had feedback from the team on your leadership? If so, what have you changed, if anything?

▎ If you could have an ideal team, what is the highest level of achievement you would like to see?

From answering these questions, have you noticed anything? What mood has this evoked in you? One of hope, sadness, frustration? Map your mood on the mood meter (Figure 3.2).

Now look at each individual in your team.

EXERCISE 9.2

Can you answer some of the following questions?

Team member	What do they do well?	What are their areas for development?	What are their main motivators?	Can you list their values?	What mood do they bring to the group?
Mike					
Angela					
Dorothy					
Jonathan					
Ian					
Sarah					
David					
Matt					

Evaluating your team for signs of engagement or disengagement

There are many ways to spot if your team are disengaged. Similar to the Plutchik model mentioned in Step Two of this book, disengagement happens gradually in stages so you can spot the signs early on if you use your skills in recognising emotional responses in others. Some broad indicators include: arriving late, absenteeism, deliberately elusive behaviour, unjustified animosity toward management, declining appearance and isolation.

> There are many ways to spot if your team are disengaged

The three stages of disengagement

However, on a stage basis, the first stage of disengagement tends to manifest as a reduction in performance. Here are the stages outlined in more detail.

- **Stage one.** If you are extremely diligent and astute in how you know and engage with your team, you will spot this very early on. This will happen if you take the time to walk around and understand what motivates and drives people, as mentioned in Step One. You will spot a change in morale very quickly, which can often be prompted by such things as a disappointment or something that has upset them internally or in their own lives.

- **Stage two.** This will be slightly more obvious, as the person's behaviour will change and can be visible as withdrawal, agitation or discontentment. This stage is almost irreversible as they have mentally started to leave the organisation. If you are interested in making sure that the employee remains in the organisation, you will need to work hard to demonstrate your commitment to win them back. This can take a lot of energy and effort on your part to turn the beginnings of their mistrust back to a place where they can recommit.

▌ **Stage three.** At this point, the employee has mentally left, given up and is simply biding their time until the next opportunity comes along. This is a dangerous stage, as not only are they about to leave but they may also be on a crusade to execute revenge on the organisation for making them feel this way by causing lots of disruption.

Engaging a team – values and motivators

A 2014 study of 142 countries by Gallup (a large consultancy that delivers analytics and advice to help leaders and organisations) (Adkins, 2015) found that just 13 per cent of employees worldwide are engaged at work. This basically means that 1 in 8 workers of a population of 180 million worldwide are psychologically committed to their organisation and are making positive contributions. This is quite a depressing set of statistics for leaders and managers of teams. There is a real responsibility to try to ensure that you engage your teams and design an environment and set of targets that are stretching, interesting and productive. Our experience working with executives suggests to us that people are disengaged usually because they are treated not as humans with underlying emotions but as rational robots who simply show up for work and satisfy endless deadlines and pressures with no consideration for how they may be feeling or what they need to make life a little more bearable.

In Step One we discussed the importance of understanding your own values. In order to build an engaged team you need to take some time to understand the values of each of your team, if possible. This will help you understand what motivates and drives each individual. It will be utterly different for some and similar for others. For example, if you have a longstanding member of your team who intimately knows their job, the business and enjoys their work, they may have zero ambition in terms of seeking promotion and additional status. They simply want to collect their pay and go home at a certain hour every evening in order to put their children to bed. Their values are deeply rooted in the importance of spending time with their family. There is absolutely nothing wrong with such behaviour but, if you have someone else on the team who is completely the opposite, then you may make some unfavourable comparisons. For example, you may also have someone on the same team who works from early morning until late into the evening and has hinted that they have ambitions for your job when it becomes available. Their values might be steeped in high ambition and a strong work ethos. These two sets of values may seem polar opposites, but the intentions of both individuals are good. Therefore, how can you tap into these values to ensure that these two individuals stay motivated and find some commonality so they can get on with the task at hand and complete it successfully? You must keep both engaged at an individual level but also find a way that will engage them as a team.

> You need to take some time to understand the values of each of your team

CASE STUDY

The engaged team

A divisional manager of a global health insurance company that we worked with in the past asked all of her team (thirty individuals) to share a minimum of three of their values with the group. She collated all ninety values and searched for common themes. She conducted a factor analysis and eight values remained, which collectively represented those of the team. These values were published and she organised an offsite meeting with her team to examine the organisational strategy and think of a way to localise it to their department using the eight values that they had identified.

The team wholly engaged with the process as they felt that the approach would encapsulate how they liked to work. They subsequently subdivided the strategy into projects that they could work on both as a large team and then as small teams. When we went to visit their open plan offices, we observed there were posters of the team's eight values on display and as screensavers on their computer monitors. On reflection, they were one of the most engaged teams we had ever met and the CEO was struck by their endless initiative and enthusiasm. They also forged new allegiances with each other as, although they were different in profile, like the two people described earlier, they still shared a common bond in terms of understanding what were the drivers and motivators of the team. This also allowed the individuals to remain emotionally balanced as they were satisfying what was important to them and weren't putting aside their own values every day when they walked through the door to work.

True North Groups

Other leaders who have adopted a similar approach include Bill George, who was the CEO of Medtronic when it grew from a $1.1 billion to a $60 billion company. He acknowledged the importance of encouraging peers to form small intimate groups and talk openly about personal and professional issues as well as about their beliefs, values and principles in a confidential setting. He believed that these groups evolved into very important support mechanisms for individuals who could share in and confide in their peers, hence helping them to recognise, understand and manage their emotions. All very emotionally agile abilities. He and his colleague Doug Baker wrote a fascinating book called *True North Groups* which documents the process of forming these groups and how they can benefit the individual and organisation. They describe a range of group functions including: a nurturer, a grounding rod, a truth teller and a mirror. When they are functioning well as a group, all of the members are caring coaches and thoughtful mentors. Perhaps it might be useful to set up a True North Group for yourself and some fellow leaders within your organisation?

What is a high-performing team?

In order to create a high-performing team, it is useful to figure out what such a team might look like generically and then individualise it to your own organisation.

A high-performing team:

▌ Achieves outstanding results and usually surpasses previous targets.

▌ Usually pursues a goal that is stretching and inspirational for its team members.

▌ Has team members who are all fully engaged with enthusiasm and energy to achieve and surpass expectations.

▌ Will often describe its work as invigorating, inspirational and life-changing.

These attributes may seem elusive to you now, but the case study below offers some insight into how skills in emotional agility can help you to move from a low- to a high-performing team.

CASE STUDY

Turning a low-performing team into a high-performing team using EA

In the past, we, as facilitators, worked with a small team (ten individuals) from the technology sector who came to us for a leadership development programme. As part of their first module, the group were tasked by their senior management to build a strategy to help the organisation regain focus for the next ten years and beyond. The team was small but seemed determined to do a good job. The group began their task with great enthusiasm and brainstormed with vigour. The ideas flowed and the group became very excited about three possibilities that emerged from the initial conversations. The facilitators then suggested that the group could possibly narrow down their range of ideas to one or two feasible projects that could be taken on by five members of two teams and continue to work on the projects between module one and two. They all agreed to this and vowed to return to us for module two a number of months later with a lot of the work completed. However, on the last day of the first module, word started to filter through that the organisation, which had been executing a voluntary redundancy programme, had accepted the resignation of two of the team who had secretly applied for the programme. There was huge surprise among the team and the dynamic in the room immediately changed. The trust and good humour that had existed earlier immediately vanished.

When the group went back to their organisation after the programme, they simply fell apart. No one had any time for meetings, so the projects kept getting pushed back and no progress was made. By the time they arrived for module two, the projects had not only stalled completely but the group were completely rethinking the title of the projects. They asked for the module to be paused so they could focus on this very important work. The group was now reduced to seven (because of the two voluntary redundancies and one involuntary one) and were absolutely dysfunctional. A leader had emerged from the group – a very weak one functionally but a master of manipulation and bluster. He had a lot of the psychopathic tendencies outlined in Step Six but the remainder of the group, who were in fact more intelligent than him, seemed to defer to him due to their need for reassurance. For two days the facilitators watched the group flip flop about and get nowhere. Their ideas, which were led by the poor and incapable leader, were weak and if presented to their senior leaders would have made the team look very bad. After some time, the facilitators started to spend time with each member of the group to figure out what was going on. It emerged that there was a huge amount of fear overshadowing the project as they were concerned that they would be the next victim to lose their job, especially if they presented a poor project to the senior team. It turned out they were so preoccupied with this fear that they could not even conceive of a good idea. Their creativity and any innovative ideas were completely hijacked.

Working on some of the more advanced thinkers, the facilitators tried to free up some of the worries by exploring the worst possible scenario with the team members. It worked. A number of hours later, one or two of the quieter and more intelligent members of the team slowly started to raise their voices and their ideas began to flow. The leader tried to quash them as he felt his power slipping away but the facilitators made space for the emerging leaders of the team and their ideas finally won through. The team ended up going from a highly dysfunctional group into a much higher performing team who were able to conceive a project that would help the organisation save at least £1 million in the short term. They presented their project to the senior management at the next strategy meeting and it was wholly supported and a recommendation granted that it should be rolled out globally across the organisation.

This case study is a great example of how a team, which should be functioning well, i.e. one with all the necessary capabilities, intelligence and resources, became completely hopeless due to some emotions that stopped their progress and ability to think. If you are managing a group like this, then there are a number of steps you can take to increase their performance:

How to increase team performance

1. **Create a vision.** Most teams can only work at a high functionality for short periods of time as the body and mind simply cannot sustain the energy needed to perform at such a level. Therefore, for any team to succeed, you must create a vision which they can work towards, i.e. build something that is, ultimately, part of a bigger picture, or stage it so that they can see a route to the finish line. The vision needs to be clear but will be appealing in different ways to different individuals, depending on their own values and how they like to be appealed to. It is worth exploring if they have left-brain tendencies and therefore enjoy a logical and linear set of instructions or are mostly right-brained and attracted by inspirational and aspirational outcomes, which are hard to define. The best vision a team can work towards is one they create themselves and therefore own.

2. **Build a heterogeneous team.** The members of most high-performing teams have a variety of skills and expertise with different backgrounds and are of different ages. Unfortunately, a lot of organisations tend to resource departments with people of similar backgrounds to those already in situ, which they think will work well and fit in well with the rest of the company. This may make for an easy life initially but you simply create a group of clones who will become homogenous and spend most of their time in group think. It takes real leadership to get

a disparate group of people to work together, while still understanding and respecting each other and finding optimal ways of cooperating. Most innovation comes from differences of opinion and ideas that can find a way to be translated into quirky projects.

3. **Use emotional agility.** It is essential at all times to ensure you are observing the dynamics of the group and regularly checking in to see what is happening with each member of the team. Just one person can completely destroy the performance abilities. In this instance it was a combination of an unstable organisational environment/ context that unsettled the whole group. This, coupled with a change in the dynamic and the emergence of an incapable but smooth-talking leader who took the group in completely the wrong direction, destabilised the group. Using your skills in emotional agility, you should now be able to assess the collective mood of the team, and of each individual, and analyse the context in which they are working to ensure that nothing will or has destabilised their task. The facilitators mentioned above are experienced in spotting behaviours that, on the surface, appear quite strange but always have an underlying dimension driven by certain emotions.

IN SUMMARY

Making the most of your team can be one of the most challenging jobs you have as a leader. From reading this chapter, you should, with some time, effort and reflection, slowly build up some useful knowledge on what motivates your team, their values and what you want to achieve from this group of people. It is evident that the rewards are great if you invest time, energy and trust in them. Good, clear, stretching goals will help them to achieve great things for your department and organisation.

10

Using EA to enhance creativity and innovation

Successful and innovative firms that began as a creative idea

The outputs from creativity and innovation are evident from many organisations that have emerged over the last number of years, often in the wake of the decline of other markets and products. In Step One of this book we spoke of Tony Hsieh, CEO and founder of Zappos, an online shoe retailer that was bought by Amazon for $1 billion in 2009 – an organisation that had achieved so much because of its named passion and values. Another innovative company that arose from the ashes of the global financial crisis is the hugely successful Funding Circle, which uses peer-to-peer technology to connect small businesses with lenders; it provides cheaper finance than high street banks without assuming the credit risk of holding loans on balance sheets. This company found a gap in the banking sector, which had almost entirely disappeared as an industry due to the lending policies of selling loans to those who could simply not afford them for extortionate profits. Such a creative move by the founders of Funding Circle meant they appealed to an audience whose mistrust in banks had grown and were desperate for an alternative. Since its launch in 2010, Funding Circle has gained 38,000 investors who have lent money through the site, including individuals, financial institutions and the

UK Government. Collectively, they have invested $1 billion in 8,000 businesses around the world, lending $80 million each month.

> **Creativity and innovation are the drivers of many successful contemporary businesses**

Another example of creativity and innovation in action, valued at $2.5 billion and used by an estimated 50,000 to 60,000 people a night, is Airbnb. Before Airbnb became a giant online marketplace for sharing homes and spaces, it began as a couple of air beds on a floor in San Francisco. In 2008, Brian Chesky and his co-founders, desperate for cash but confident they had an idea worth pursuing, went into the cereal business. They made special-edition Cheerios boxes for both presidential candidates, called Obama O's and Cap'n McCains, with hot glue and cardboard, selling several hundred items for tens of thousands of dollars when investors refused to give them money. They succeeded in their efforts and are now the 'go to' for accommodation for travellers all over the world. What these companies have in common is that their founders had an idea that was fuelled by their core values (outlined in Step One) that included passion, determination and optimism. This, combined with the help of some good investors, succeeded in turning their innovative ideas into huge global entities. These companies are inspirational for those leaders who are hoping to create and build the next big thing through the promotion of creativity and innovation.

What is innovation?

In order to really create an innovative work environment, it is useful to know what innovation can and does look like in organisations. Some academics describe it as the term used to explain *the creation of a new product or the rejuvenation of existing processes or products.* There have been many studies of innovation in organisations and its effect on performance. Some studies found that innovative firms out-perform non innovators, and these better-performing firms are more likely to further innovate and subsequently devote more resources to innovation (Cainelli *et al.*, 2006). They describe it as a self-reinforcing mechanism. Camelo Ordaz, Hernandez-Lara and Valle Cabrera (2005) devised three stages of innovation that illustrate the multitude of definitions of the concept. These are: 'innovation in process', which examines the creative activities in motion, 'innovation in results', which examines the creation of new products or patents in the business, and 'innovation status', which examines innovation as a built-in attribute of the organisation. West (2002) describes innovation as a two-stage process often referred to as ambidextrous. The first stage involves exploration, where employees can take risks, experiment and enjoy flexibility while uncovering new and varying phenomena of interest. The second stage is where employees work within an environment where exploitation is valued and where they are encouraged to follow rules that enhance efficiency (Shipton *et al.*, 2006, p. 4).

EXERCISE 10.1

How innovative is your organisation?

▌ Think about the two-stage process described above.

▌ Now plot your organisation against these stages.

▌ Would you say your organisation is innovative or not?

What types of firms are most innovative?

The size of organisation doesn't appear to have much bearing on whether it is innovative or not. Ironically, larger firms are often proportionately less innovative than smaller firms, which is rather surprising at first glance, because one would imagine that larger firms will have greater resources for research and development (R&D). However, studies like that by Acs and Audretsch (1988) found that the number of innovations in an industry increases with R&D expenditures, but at a decreasing rate. The reason for this is that highly creative individuals can become discouraged in large R&D laboratory operations, while small firms are usually cost conscious, and the same project might be conducted with less waste of resources.

Context is also very important when considering innovation, as innovation in service firms is very different from innovation in manufacturing firms. When Tether (2005) studied three thousand firms, he found substantial differences in how manufacturing and service firms innovate. He found that service firms are more likely to collaborate with suppliers and customers, while manufacturing firms stress the importance of R&D spend and links with universities. Service industries are likely to focus on soft skills, whereas manufacturing industries value the more technical skills. He also states that service firms are known to constantly adapt and change their offerings to provide solutions to changing and differentiated customer requirements. This often leads to the co-production of services, where the client and firm work together to create an innovative and dynamic solution, which makes it difficult to measure the true source of the innovation activity. Due to the uniqueness of the stakeholder inputs of service firm innovation, Coombs and Miles (2000) state that innovation activities in service firms require newer measures and approaches to capture innovation than those developed to measure innovation in manufacturing firms.

Emotional agility and creativity

The role of emotions and emotional states are hugely significant in stimulating creativity and innovation. A prolific academic on the subject of creativity, Amabile (1988), found that positive emotions promote increased creativity in some contexts and emotionally intelligent leaders explain significant variance of creativity dimensions. In a separate study of ninety Indian executives, managerial innovation was also positively related to emotional intelligence (Yuvaraj and Srivastava, 2007). In examining the role of emotion during the creative design process, and the emotion management of teams and clients, in two hundred architectural firms in Europe (Fleming, 2012), a number of links between emotion and creativity emerged. The results of this study offer us a means to illustrate how the steps of emotional agility can help promote creativity for you as a leader.

EXERCISE 10.2

How to use EA to promote creativity

1. Recognise and tap into your own emotions for inspiration

The first finding is linked to Step Two of this book, where the ability to recognise emotions in oneself must first happen in order to tune into that creativity. Some architects in the study spoke of the importance of finding inspiration from music, culture and other architecture to help evoke emotions which, in turn, inspired creative thoughts.

2. Manage your own unwanted emotions

In the study of architects, it was found that wonderfully creative moods were sometimes interrupted by the organisational demands or difficult clients and peers due to functional and resource-driven outcome pressures. This often evoked emotions such as frustration or anger, which, if you encounter as a leader, must be managed in order not to overshadow any creative thoughts you may have. These can both hijack the immediate creativity and repress future creativity, which is an essential aspect of the work of any architect – or of you as leader.

3. Recognise the emotions of others

The flip side of being able to evoke creativity is that creative types, who work mostly from their right-brain abilities, can often feel emotions more deeply or be more aware of them. This can result in them being more emotionally charged and sometimes resistant to the rationality and process being imposed upon them by their managers. Their leaders must be able to both recognise the team's behavioural tendencies and delicately manage the emotional difficulties that inevitably arise. Your job as leader is to watch for the least intense versions of these emotions, using the Plutchik model, and catch them before they evolve into something greater and unmanageable.

4. Manage the emotions of others

As discussed in Step Six, when managing people, you inevitably meet a lot of emotional responses, some of them unpredictable. For architects, they also have the added dimension of dealing with their client's emotions during their house project. This can be as a result of the financial and emotional investment that clients make when they decide to erect or alter a building. Architects find themselves regularly consoling and reassuring the client through doubts they may have over the project, or the fears of extraordinary creative dimensions within a brief. When you are managing many stakeholders with diverse needs during a creative process, it may unleash some unwanted or unpredicted emotions – therefore, you may need to really tap into your emotion management abilities to keep them on track. This is absolutely necessary to ensure that the rational needs of the firm and client come first in order to complete projects in a timely and cost-effective manner.

5. Create and manage a mood to help inspire

Once you can tap into your own emotions, it was found that certain moods could provoke inspiration and, for the architects studied, enhanced the creative process. Using the mood meter, you can move people from one quadrant to another in order to find the mood that optimises and supports creativity. Now plot your team's current collective mood on the mood meter. How creative can they be in this mood?

6. Introduce physical movement and activity

Think of a time when you had to solve a particularly difficult or puzzling problem. The most effective thing to do is to step away, and possibly get some sleep so that the unconscious thought process can continue without stress. It is often in the performance of semi-automatic or physical activities like swimming and walking that people are at their most creative, as it provokes the left and right brain to make connections that can often lead to the best form of decision making.

Physical spaces and creativity

Other instigators of creativity are the physical spaces where people work. In fact, the role of physical space to promote creativity cannot be overestimated. The power of surroundings and how they impact on the human body and mind is often the most overlooked reason why innovation and creativity has ceased in organisations. Think of the place where you have your best ideas. Is it at your desk or in the innovation room at work? Probably neither. It is usually to be found in the least likely of places such as the shower, on a running trail or walking home. Most people, if they are lucky, have a place they can go to either to get away from it all or simply to immerse themselves in some distraction to release their day-to-day worries and anxieties. In reality, everyone should have a place that makes them feel safe, happy and secure. A place where they can either think and reflect, and process and allow their minds to settle back into a neutral state or, alternatively, a place that is highly stimulating and provokes our thoughts beyond the status quo. What you must remember is that the make-up of your physical environment has a huge influence on your moods, as they will affect your physiological state.

Think of the place where you have your best ideas

EXERCISE 10.3

Where do you go to be creative?

Think about a physical place that you enjoy going to. Is it your home, your local woods, art gallery, coffee shop, noisy pub or your bedroom?

- Describe it physically. Is it bright, dark, large or small?
- Can you relax and let go there? What kind of thoughts do you have once you get there?
- Think about your current office or the work environment of your team. Are they in a place that is conducive to being creative? Do they have their own offices? Or are they in an open-plan office in cubicles with headsets on?

In order to stimulate creativity amongst teams and work colleagues, a large number of factors have to be present. These include: purposeful relationships, trust, openness, a risk-taking environment, an inspiring leader who helps them to both manage and embrace difference. There has been scant thought given to how most organisations are structured or built to enhance this type of activity. At Ashridge, we have set up our learning spaces in ways that encourage movement and freedom and utilise all of the space both in the classroom environment and beyond, whether it is walking tracks, well-placed benches, tennis courts or places to sit on the lawn. The participants feel safe and free to chat and experiment with their colleagues while in a state of relaxed learning or in the throes of problem solving. Understandably, you may be in a context where you cannot indulge in such freedom, but it is worth exploring how you might create such an environment to inspire creativity. In the study mentioned earlier, some architects have opened up their studios to encourage all of the senior partners and associates to work in an open-plan environment. This studio environment appears to be the preferred choice for some architects, as they are all in one room working together, which tends to generate accidental cross-fertilisation of ideas. Communication is also enriched, as one architect describes:

> 'We work in an open-plan office, we all sit near each other and we are talking all the time. It is very difficult for one person to keep track of every detail, so when someone puts down the phone, we might say: "And you know something else happened which might affect X, or the client said this or the engineer said the other." We are always communicating, it is hugely important.'

A move away from the more traditional organisational structure into studio and open-plan working environments can encourage team innovative behaviours to emerge, allowing the transfer of knowledge around the firm. In a survey of UK architectural firms, by NESTA (2009), they found that innovation is mostly produced through teamwork, where internal and external partners with varying skill sets collaborate. However, for those who are more introvert, some alone time in a non-open-plan office is where the creativity happens. Susan Cain's book *Quiet* offers us a real insight into how people with a preference for introversion like to work and she is also a consultant interior designer for those wishing to build and create office spaces for introverts.

Blockers of creativity

Finally, there are a few blockers of creativity that you as a leader can choose to reduce or increase, depending on how much you value the promotion of creativity and innovation in your organisation:

1. No vision for the team or organisation.

2. Poor or non-inspiring leadership behaviours.

3. Endless focus on performance/operational activities.

4. Lack of big picture or strategic thinking.

5. No resources (or head space) for people to think or act freely.

6. Lack of trust between you and your team.

EXERCISE 10.4

How to start the creative process with your team

Now put together a plan of how you will begin the process of evoking creativity or innovation first in yourself and then in your team.

Here are some questions to get you started:

▌ What would you like to achieve?

▌ What is your vision? Imagine it clearly – draw or write about the final outcome you can imagine.

▌ Think about how you might inspire those around you to engage in such activity.

▌ Who do you want to be involved? Why would this excite them? Which of their values does this appeal to?

▌ What do you need to change or do to start the process?

▌ What is your timeframe?

Once you have established what it is you want to achieve, then you can use all the skills of EA to create the environment and the mood to make that happen.

IN SUMMARY

This chapter demonstrates how to create a work environment using EA to enable people to think freely and come up with creative ideas. It illustrates how creativity has led to some company successes, what innovation actually means and how we can measure it. You should now be able to use the steps of emotional agility to promote creativity and innovation in your work as leader and in your team. The chapter has highlighted blockers to creativity and offers some exercises as to how you can begin the process of encouraging innovation and creativity in yourself and your teams.

Managing change using EA

When considering change in your life, department or organisation, it is good to understand first, what type of change you are experiencing and, second, the impact of this change on your own behaviour, decision making and that of your team. Whether your change is re-engineering, rightsizing, restructuring, cultural change or turnaround, you must consider how you can engage your teams and realisers of change to make it happen. Kotter (1996) suggests that you know you have made a big step forward 'when you see people, lots of people, raise their hands, rather than pointing fingers'. Engendering a mood that will engage people rather than frustrate them is a key ingredient to successful change. You can do this by engaging people early on in the change process and encouraging them to help you collectively build the vision and understand what and how they can add to the change. Being emotionally agile is a key skill to help you successfully navigate the minefield of change as you now have skills in identifying emotions and in understanding the depth and, possibly, the source of people's reactions. Once people are given time to get used to a new paradigm and are offered a forum to channel their fears (unfounded or not) before being asked to execute any required initiatives, they will respond very differently from the way they would if forced into a change situation.

Personal change

There are many types of change that people experience throughout their lifetime. Personal change can happen when you experience a disruption in your life or when something ends and/or begins. This can be as simple as moving home, losing a loved one through grief or separation or adding to your family. Any type of change can cause a disruption to your exiting mental map. When change happens, you do not have any neural pathways set up to deal with the new event so it can evoke a sense of uncertainty and a feeling of loss as to what to do next. Your primitive brain kicks into action and you can become utterly frozen with fear or step up and face the change and create new neural pathways as quickly as you can. Neither response is incorrect but can affect the length of time it takes you to emerge from the effects of the change stimulus.

CASE STUDY

Dealing with loss

Melanie was thirty-five years old when her father died. Her father was a strong character and their family always looked to him for guidance and assurance. He had been diagnosed with terminal cancer the previous year and, although the family had known the outcome was bleak, they stoically carried on, almost in the pretence that, if they didn't acknowledge it, it might not happen. Her father was not one for sentimentality and, although he knew he was dying, did not speak about it with the family, so they also stayed silent. As his health began to decline, everyone rallied around him and his last request to die in his own home was facilitated by the love and assistance of his family and carers.

The day before her father died, Melanie discovered she was pregnant with her first child. She was absolutely thrilled but the emotion was mixed with huge melancholy that her wonderful father would not be around to see this new baby arrive into the world. Sitting at his bedside, she told him the news, but he was very weak and could barely speak an acknowledgement. The following day, he passed away surrounded by his family and Melanie thought that she too, at that moment, would die from grief. She felt utterly bereft and bewildered but tried to stay strong in order to make the appropriate funeral arrangements. During the funeral service, she found some comfort in hearing all the wonderful stories that her father's friends and acquaintances shared with the family and how much they would all miss him. When the funeral was over, she spent a week with her family while they tried to come to terms with the great loss in their world. The house was so empty without him. Although, in reality, he had not been tall in stature, it felt like a giant had left their world and they all wandered about wondering what to do in his absence. Her mother tackled the domestic administration, changing the name on the household bills and immersing herself in many practical tasks.

It was soon time for Melanie to return to work and she decided to throw herself into a new role that was offered to her soon after her return. She spent long days and evenings at work and was highly stimulated by the role. She cried a lot but was encouraged by her growing bump and the anticipation of a new life arriving in the world. When she finally gave birth to her son, she was utterly overwhelmed by emotions. There was a mixture of euphoria, trepidation, bewilderment and grief. The last arrived like a tidal wave. It utterly engulfed her and she was paralysed with it. There were times when she could barely look after her new baby as she was so devastated by the loss of her father. She endlessly thought about her father and, upon waking every morning, would weep uncontrollably for ten minutes before she could even attempt to get dressed. Her partner supported her in the best way that he could, but it was incredibly difficult as he was also getting used to this new and helpless little baby depending on them both for all of his needs.

It took Melanie some time to realise that she needed some help. She reluctantly arranged some time with a bereavement counsellor who helped her talk through her emotions and understand what was happening to her. It was scary for Melanie, as she felt so very out of control. She had felt in control her whole life and it was so strange not knowing the answer or knowing what the right thing to do was. It appeared that nothing made her feel better and she didn't know how to make these terrible feelings go away. When Melanie spent time with her family, there was no discussion about her father, just continued silence. She really wanted to talk about him, acknowledge how much she missed him, but the cue from her siblings was one of silence and an unspoken rule not to bring it up. It was as if, once they acknowledged it, they would all drown in grief. It made for unhappy visits home, and the sight of his chair or his shoes was too much for Melanie to bear, so she stopped visiting as regularly, as it somehow made her feel worse.

After a number of months had passed, someone at work gave her the name of a local therapist who combined cognitive hypnotherapy with acupuncture, which had a huge impact on Melanie. After a number of treatments, she started to feel brighter and more optimistic. The treatment worked for her and she responded really well. It is now just over two years since her father died and, although the magnitude of her feelings is still acute, she is learning how to cope in a world without him and enjoys telling her son all about his grandfather. It will take some time for her to fully come to terms with the fact that her father is gone and she will never see him again. She has had to transition from being the child of her father into being a parent for her son.

Melanie's story is one of personal grief and may seem out of place in a book about leadership, but it does highlight that all human beings will face some sort of deep and personal loss of a family member or friend in their life. These events can have enormous impact, and some people simply do not recover, so that the impact triggers a multitude of consequences across other areas of their lives. As we saw from the banker breakdown case study (in Chapter 5), emotions that are unresolved can fester and manifest and wreak havoc with physical and emotional states. Supressing the emotions may seem easier to begin with, but Melanie found out, after the birth of her son, nine months after her father died, that the grief was still there waiting to be dealt with. In TA terms, her Adult ego state needed to find a new way to exist in the world without her father. Her Child ego state was craving a parent who was no longer present to advise or guide her through life, so she had to begin building a new existence outside of her Child ego state, which would allow her to transcend into Adult ego state and, ultimately, be a parent to her son. If you have experienced what Melanie has gone through, you may or may not recognise her reaction, as everyone has an individual response to grief. There is no formula, no advice that you can take from anyone that will help you to best navigate your way through it. Elisabeth Kübler-Ross's change curve model suggests that people go through seven stages of emotion when they lose someone or something close to them, which she outlines as follows:

1. Shock or disbelief.

2. Denial.

3. Anger.

4. Bargaining.

5. Guilt.

6. Depression.

7. Acceptance and hope.

It is important to remember that these stages are not in chronological order, but can happen in any array and, for some people, might not happen at all. The Kübler-Ross change curve illustrates these seven stages, plotted against morale and time.

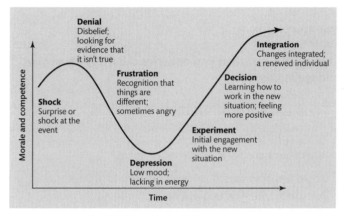

FIGURE 11.1 The Kübler-Ross change curve

Source: Kubler-Ross, E., *On Death and Dying: What the dying have to teach doctors, nurses, clergy and their own families*, Scribner Book Company, 2014.

Kübler-Ross's model offers a means to understand the types of emotions that occur during a period of loss and grief. Indeed, these stages can be mirrored during less important change events in people's lives but the reactions can follow the same curve. Using the steps of emotional agility, it is useful to spot these emotions and understand that there is a slow and purposeful route through these emotions in order for them to be properly processed and dealt with. The biggest mistake is for someone to skip over some of the stages in order to come out of the dark periods as the emotion will reappear at some later stage when a non-related event triggers it back into action when it is least expected. Therefore, no matter how painful or hopeless it may feel at the time, it is important to slowly navigate the process so that healing and, ultimately, acceptance can occur for the individual. Managing something as huge as grief will require a level of inner strength and resource which is far greater than managing a less intense emotion that may be caused by an event at work or a person discounting your values.

EXERCISE 11.1

Think of a time when you experienced a large personal change in your life

▌ Can you describe what happened?

▌ How did you initially respond?

▌ What emotions did you experience, if any?

▌ If time has now passed and you can now look back, can you summarise how you responded?

▌ How did this personal change subsequently impact upon or affect you as a person?

Professional change

Although personal events may be very different, the effects of change on your professional life can also have a big impact on your emotional state and that of your team. Most of the executives we meet have found their way to us because they either need to change something at work and don't know how to or have tried to change their department or organisation and maybe it hasn't gone so well. Most modern businesses go through a business life cycle that demands continuous change and responses to the markets in which they operate. The model is illustrated and explained in Figure 11.2.

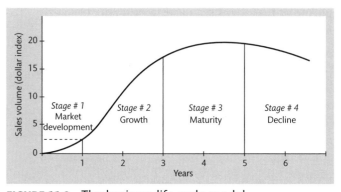

FIGURE 11.2   The business life cycle model

Source: Levitt, T., 'Exploit the business life cycle', *Harvard Business Review*, 1969.

The business life cycle is akin to the life cycle in nature, which is evident throughout the seasons and requires various resources and environments in order to thrive during each phase and move on to the next one. Businesses are no different. This cycle, which was first suggested in the mid-twentieth century, is still visible in lots of contemporary organisations but is, of course, subject to some exceptions for certain modern businesses. The stages of the business life cycle are now explained.

> The business life cycle is akin to the life cycle in nature

▌ **Development stage.** This is often the beginning of a business when someone conceives a creative idea that is fuelled by a strong passion and belief driven from an individual's core values (which we discussed in Chapter 1) and perhaps some emotions that have stimulated creativity (which we discussed in Chapter 10). The market is assessed for feasibility at this point and subsequent funding and resources are sought to bring the idea to fruition stage.

▌ **Introduction stage.** Once feasibility, funding and legitimacy have been established, the business will make its first sale and continuously adjust the product or service to ensure that they are responding accurately to the market. This is an exciting and daunting time for the founder(s) and evokes a whole myriad of emotions fuelled by adrenaline and utter belief that the business can and will work.

▌ **Growth stage.** When the business finds its niche in the market and sales start to increase, the business starts to become more complicated and requires more complex structures to support the production or generation of increased sales, which may include the hiring of more employees to cope with increased demands. Some businesses go through a rapid growth phase and imagine that the business will continue to expand in its current form at this rate indefinitely.

▌ **Maturity stage.** When any business establishes itself in a market and becomes successful within that market, it will also attract the attention of other similar businesses who will enter the same market. Competitors will endeavour to take market share by pursing any number of tactics, which may include a lower price or increase in marketing or promotional activities. In addition, consumers who once were a big fan of a certain product or service may now have moved into a different market which is being served by a new start-up organisation prompted by a different set of needs. The big challenge at this point is to decide if the business in its current form can continue or whether it needs to change in order to survive and grow in new markets.

▌ **Decline stage.** At this point the business has substantially reduced its market share and, potentially, has made the difficult decision to shed some of its employees in order to reduce the costs of running the business. The founders may still cling tightly to the notion that the business proposition is a wonderful idea and may display confusion as to what has happened. This is a crucial point for businesses to either end what has brought their success and create something new from the ashes or adjust the product or service in the hope that they will still experience some sales and recover.

If you compare the life cycle of a business to the seven stages of grief, which we outlined earlier in the chapter, you will see that they occur almost in reverse. One is about facing decline and trying to recover and regrow from the experience while the other flows in the opposite direction.

Dealing with change

As evidenced by the business life cycle outlined above, there is, at a minimum, a requirement for continuous or incremental change in order to remain successful and survive the fickle demands of consumers and markets from growth to maturity. Before or during the decline stage, most organisations have to go through a rapid or transformational change in order to either survive their new context or rapidly adjust their product or service to recover market share. We meet executives who are either struggling to move from one phase of the life cycle to the other or others who are in decline stage and do not know what to do. Their mental maps, which have got them so far in their professional careers, are no longer useful to help them figure out what to do next. Most express a willingness to embrace change, but the reality is different. They feel scared of the unknown and find that their teams resist any suggestion of real change with force and obstinacy. One model, which is helpful to explore in order to understand the reactions of individuals during a change process, is the transition model, created by change consultant William Bridges.

Bridges transition model

This transition model addresses the difference between change, which happens *to* people, and transition, which is what happens *inside* of people, as they experience change.

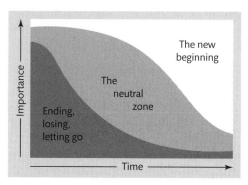

FIGURE 11.3   The Bridges transition model

Source: Bridges, W., *Making Transitions: Making the Most of Change*, 3rd edn, Brealey Publishing, 2009. Courtesy of Nicholas Bealey Publishing (UK and Commonwealth) and Da Capo Press, a member of The Perseus Books Group (rest of the world).

According to Bridges, there are three stages of transition when people go through change:

Stage 1: Ending, losing and letting go

The first stage of transition is what people experience when change is happening and they have to say goodbye to something that is very familiar and comforting and that is no longer relevant or cannot survive the change. This stage is often the most difficult, as people have just been presented or ambushed with the change and can have quite a visceral reaction when their world has been disrupted. Resistance can come in the form of people threatening to leave the organisation, sabotage the change or utterly resist what is happening. As you have read (in Chapter 2), your ability to identify emotions is very important at this point, as the shock of having to let go of something can trigger a whole range of emotions within the person experiencing the change. As outlined (in Chapter 4), the emotion that the individual experiences and expresses can irrationally arrive as an unrelated, but deeply held, emotional response from childhood, which has now been triggered by the current event. Bridges suggests that people experience some of the following emotions during this stage: fear, denial, anger, sadness, disorientation, frustration, uncertainty and a sense of loss. The emotions that are displayed may be explicit but may also be in the less intense form as per the Plutchik model (Figure 2.1). Although your main task as leader may be to successfully implement the new change process, an even more important role is to pay close attention to the emotions that are emerging, as your ability to deal with these emotions in a sensitive and timely way will, ultimately, help you in the achievement of your eventual change goal.

> Pay close attention to the emotions which are emerging during the change process

Guiding people through stage 1

Your first job as leader is to acknowledge the emotion and accept the resistance in whatever way it comes. This involves a number of steps, which chapters 3, 5 and 6 will help you to navigate.

First, you must *pay attention* to the individual and either assess how they are feeling about the change or, if you have an established relationship, ask them. Some people in your team will demonstrate overt emotional displays or dissatisfaction, whereas others will firmly maintain their emotions in the hidden area of the Johari Window (Figure 3.1).

Second, if you are able to uncover some of the emotions in response to change, *allow people the time and space* to process what has happened. Your role as leader at this point is to listen empathetically and be honest in your communication about what is going to happen as a result of the change.

Third, spend time helping your team understand how relevant their current skills, knowledge and experience will be in helping to navigate this new environment. *Provide reassurance* that you will help them acquire whatever new skills are required, but also build on how this change can offer some new opportunities for them to develop and grow professionally.

Fourth, *create a vision for the future* and present it in a novel and engaging way, so that your team can visualise what this new world will look like and, hopefully, generate some excitement about what is possible. If there is any scope to help them shape the vision in some way, however small, give them the opportunity to do this, as it will create a sense of power and ownership that may reduce the feelings of loss.

One way to help your team through this loss is to work through an adaptation of Exercise 5.3 (in Chapter 5).

EXERCISE 11.2

Some questions to help you understand and manage your emotions during stage 1

▌ Describe the change event that is triggering an emotional response inside of you.

▌ What emotions are you experiencing as a result of this change?

▌ What is happening to your body, your mind? How are you sleeping?

▌ What do you see as the worst thing that could happen to you? Describe it in vivid detail.

▌ Is there anything that you may be happy to let go of as a result of this change?

▌ Is there anything positive that may come from this change?

▌ What would make you feel better?

▌ What are the first steps you can take to start the process of feeling a little better?

Stage 2: neutral zone

The second stage occurs when people are still feeling somewhat connected to the old normal, but they are also starting to connect to the new normal. It is a grey area, because their identity is in flux. Although you may have identified the losses and have helped them understand the emotions that they are going through, the second stage can bring much confusion and uncertainty for some. This may be because your team member has accepted that change is happening but is impatient due to the increased workload or new systems that have just been introduced. Their mental maps will have been conditioned to work in a certain way, but they now need to learn a new way of doing things, which can seem pointless and more cumbersome as they get used to something different. During this stage, Bridges suggests that people might experience: resentment, low morale and reduced productivity, anxiety about their status or identity and pessimism about the change initiative. However negative these emotions may seem, if managed well by you as leader, this stage can lead to creativity and innovation and allow people to shape new ways of working in the new environment.

Guiding people through stage 2

Although stage 2 is referred to as the neutral zone, there is still much work to be done in terms of ensuring people stay committed and focused to the change process. Your main job as leader is to demonstrate lots of patience and offer people a clear sense of direction.

Now is a good time for you to *build some clear goals* as an outcome of the vision that you have presented so that the team can work towards something tangible that will help achieve the change targets. It is also important to offer some quick wins so that the team can feel that they are actually achieving something in the new change process.

Continuously *encourage your team to talk about how they feel* and start some meetings or interactions with plotting the group on the mood meter (Figure 3.2). Feelings will evolve and you may notice that people who were keen to embrace the change can shift back into resentment. These feelings need to be listened to, understood and managed.

Regularly meet with the team to *offer feedback on how they are performing* within the new structure or regime. It is a steep learning curve for most people, and this is a crucial time to ensure that team members are effectively working within the new system and also to spot any glitches when they arise.

Ensure that you *have enough resources in place* to manage any increased workload during this period. There is nothing more demotivating than being encouraged to be part of a change initiative only to find that it just means a huge increase in an individual's workload because no one has properly mapped out the resources required to implement and embed the change.

Stage 3: The new beginning

This stage is often referred to as the new normal and usually embodies acceptance and energy. At this stage, individuals have almost fully let go of the past and have started to accept the change. If you have managed the other stages well, your team will have begun to build up some new skills to help them navigate the new systems and processes and may start to feel proud of their new achievements. The emotions that people experience at this point are: increased energy, openness and commitment to their new role. If you have remained a constant, empathetic and positive leader throughout the difficult process of change, your team will see you as a close ally and someone who has helped them through what may have been a very difficult process. As leader, there is still a lot that you can do to ensure that your team embark on this new journey and make a success of the change.

> Everyone goes through change at their own pace

Guiding people through stage 3

Continue to advocate the *setting of related goals and objectives* for both the desired change outcome and the personal development of each of your team members. Understanding their ambitions and developmental needs will allow you to channel their skills into the achievement of their personal development as well as the change project objectives.

Take some time out to celebrate the change and offer some rewards to thank the team for their efforts. You may now need to build some new teams and connect people from other departments who have never needed to work together before. This takes time, energy and commitment from both sides and it is important to conceive the best way to do this that feels authentic and real to the group.

Pay close attention to the team even during this new beginning stage. People can slip back into the previous stages if they continually meet obstacles or are ignored. Take the time to ensure the team members properly settle into this period and try not to rush anyone to this or any stage.

Use the Kübler-Ross change curve (Figure 11.1) to help you *observe what stage each member of your team* is at in terms of how they are feeling and subsequently behaving. It is worth remembering that everyone goes through change at a different pace, so you must be patient in how you manage, each individual through the process.

EXERCISE 11.3

In order to help you fully empathise with how your team might be feeling during the change process, now think of a change project that, as an employee, you were previously a part of.

▌ How was the change communicated and subsequently implemented?

▌ Was the initiative a surprise to you or expected?

▌ How did you initially respond to the proposed change?

▌ How did it make you feel?

▌ Was the transition model used to manage your reaction to the change?

▌ If so, did it help? If not, how was your response managed, if at all?

▌ On reflection, if you could have an open and honest dialogue with your manager from that time, what would you say were the highs and lows for you, personally?

▌ Was the aforementioned change project successful? That is, did it achieve what it set out to achieve?

How to introduce change using eight steps

Now that you understand the impact that change can have on individuals, you can comfortably introduce change in your team, department or organisation by following some well-considered steps. One of the most renowned authors on change, Kotter (1996), introduced eight steps to help leaders instigate and implement change in their organisations.

Step 1: Create a sense of urgency

Kotter advocates that you begin with some stimulating and controversial conversations around the need for change in the organisation. This may be the presentation of some data or statistics that legitimately show a decline in sales or some new market information that will threaten the current status of the organisation. The main aim is to encourage your team to step outside of their current thinking and provoke some conversations that will help to progress their thinking that something may need to change.

Step 2: Form a team of change champions or leaders

When you have convinced people at a superficial level that something needs to change, you need to put together a team of individuals who will help to champion and influence the need for change. These individuals may not be the most senior people in the organisation but they are the ones who have an ability to influence those around them. As with building a highly engaged team (in Chapter 10), it is important to ensure that this group of people have different skill sets and originate from various parts of the organisation.

Step 3: Create a vision for change

Like guiding your team members through stage 1 of the transition model, it is important to help people create a vision of what the future could look like as a result of this change. At this point, you can speak about the core values that will guide the change to ensure that individuals know that the purpose of the change is well thought through and has some merit and connectedness to what they already believe in.

Step 4: Communicate the vision

Create a speech or narrative that you can communicate to the team with ease, clarity and sincerity. This speech does not need to be reserved for plenary or large group meetings but can be articulated during every conversation with your team and amongst the change champions. Use your vision when speaking about current operations and how it might apply to achieving successes and wins now and in the future.

Step 5: Remove obstacles

As discussed in the stages of the transition model, it is important to pay attention to those who may have opposing feelings to the change. It is not about railroading them into your way of thinking but really listening to what they have to say and paying close attention to whether their concerns have any merit. If people are resisting due to resource constraints or poor training and development, ensure that you have properly resourced the change.

Step 6: Create short-term wins

Give people a taste of what success may look like in the short term. It will encourage a flood of positive emotions and will help people to improve their mood and hence further embrace the change in all its guises. It can help motivate the team to move to the next stage and join the change champion team, which you should be seeking to continuously expand.

Step 7: Build on the wins

Kotter warns that lots of change initiatives fail because of victory or success being called too early. He suggests the need for constant analysis of every win to ensure continuous and sustainable improvement in the long term. At this point, he also suggests refreshing your change champion teams to ensure that new ideas and key influencers are part of the embedding of the new change process.

Step 8: Anchor the changes

To ensure that change is sustainable, it must, ultimately, find its way into the core culture of the organisation. Embed the new change and values into the organisational culture and ensure that new hires are familiarised with the new processes and systems that have grown from the change initiative. Continue to speak of the progress of the change project and repeat any success stories that you hear.

Remaining emotionally agile during the change process

As discussed throughout this chapter, when people are faced with change, most feel a sense of powerlessness and helplessness as the change is happening *to* them. This can be more pronounced for more established workers, as they may have a status quo that they have quietly built up over the years. This group has huge experience of how the organisation operates and will be extremely important in ensuring that the change can be translated into a sensible operational reality. However, for newer people in the organisation, or indeed those who are younger, change can be seen as a great opportunity to increase their profile in the company and they often show extreme willingness to be part of the change. Having a variation of demographics is always healthy in an organisation, but leading them all through the change will require you to be agile in your leadership behaviours and consistently build trust with all parties. In a study of change reforms in the UK's National Health Service, Day and Lubitsh (2012) found that establishing quality relationships and building trust was the most powerful means in enabling organisational and behavioural change.

> When people are faced with change, most feel a sense of powerlessness and helplessness

This type of leadership requires lots of listening, building trust through being emotionally intelligent – which can take time. As demonstrated, these skills can be developed by leaders using methods such as coaching, traditional leadership development and by introducing action research behaviours where leaders in their own context of change use a process of repeated cycles of action and reflection. This self-awareness will help you as leader to understand that although the needs of the organisation are rational, most of the human employees are primarily emotional beings. This approach is a powerful means of transforming leaders, using intellectual, practical, experiential, tacit, emotional, expressive and intuitive activities.

IN SUMMARY

This chapter outlines the different types of change that individuals can experience and will allow you as leader to understand the reactions and responses that your team may experience as a result of introducing a change initiative. The business life cycle demonstrates that change is an inevitable part of business and needs to be embraced in order for success to prevail. The human reaction to change is also captured through the Kübler-Ross change curve, while the Bridges transition model offers a means to help your team through the change transition. Kotter's eight steps offers a useful model on how to successfully introduce change and can be a helpful tool if used in conjunction with the other aforementioned tools.

On a final note, it is always worth considering the need for change and whether your organisation is just aimlessly rationalising to demonstrate any kind of progress. Indeed, it has become very trendy over the past twenty years to follow a change strategy of lean organisations and, although it is a demonstrable way to reduce costs and demonstrate a better margin for your shareholders, there is a risk of damaging your organisation's DNA in the process. Organisations that have followed this path have, in actual fact, reduced their overall organisational life cycle, because this short-term modular approach may result in a lean organisation but one that is empty of real talent, commitment and passion. Such qualities, which prevail in most start-up organisations, are vital to maintain growth and innovation in all organisations. Therefore, when you think about change, think beyond lean and cost reduction and consider how you can create a sustainable organisation that goes beyond shareholder value and encourages your employees to engage and share their talent as a means to grow the organisation.

When you think about change, think beyond cost reduction

At Ashridge, we challenge our executives as to whether speed and high growth rates are the only way to demonstrate success. We suggest that nurturing your key stakeholders, such as your employees, suppliers, the consumer and the local community, may offer a more sustainable and longer-term recipe for success. This approach offers contemporary organisations a brave alternative to the traditional route of short-term efficiencies and the fashionable and abhorrent practices of those demonstrating how much havoc they have wreaked in their first 100 days of leadership. Leaving the final word to Kotter: 'In the end, it is not about how fast you get off the block, but how strong and fast you finish.' The antithesis of this can be found on most epitaphs of failed change initiatives.

12

Becoming a more effective and influential leader using the seven steps of EA

The contemporary leader – your challenges

I n order to write an effective book on leading, it is important to take stock of what a contemporary leader's world looks like. As a business school who works with thousands of leaders every year, we surveyed our clients, mostly senior executives, to assess what the real issues are that they, as leaders, are grappling with in post-recession times. The biggest challenges that emerged include globalisation, changing demographics, synergising acquisition capabilities to make global products and working effectively across cultures. Other issues that emerged are the building of creative and innovative environments in spite of shareholder and client demands and finally, dealing with ambiguity and complexity.

In order to cope with these demands, most of the current leadership research no longer focuses on one individual leader, but considers the role of followers, supervisors, culture, work context and citizenship behaviours. Therefore, the role of EA is a hugely important skill when you as leader need to influence all of these stakeholders and work comfortably across all of these contexts. Most of these new leadership models examine symbolic leader behaviour, inspirational messages, emotional feelings, values, individual attention and intellectual stimulation. A popular model amongst these is authentic leadership that draws from positive psychological capacities. This leads to greater leader self-awareness and regulated behaviours, which, in turn, lead to positive self-development (Luthans and Avolio, 2003). This model is one that suggests that leaders combine rationality with complementary styles of thinking, such as intuition, creativity and emotion, which encourages insight and guides comprehensive decision making – all good endorsements for the role of emotional agility in leadership.

> Effective leaders have a clearly defined vision and goal, maintain a sense of self and empower their followers

How do we define a good leader?

In order to help leaders tackle these issues, we surveyed our faculty and experts on leadership at Ashridge and externally to enquire how they might define leadership, what it is *not,* and how these views might assist leaders to increase their impact within their current and complex environments. The main theme that emerged is that *effective leaders* have a clear defined vision and goal, are real, can flex in the moment, lead from the heart and empower their followers and teams by having consistent values and by being authentic. This creates trust and commitment. These two ingredients will drive any business forward. One way to engender these skills is to use your emotional agility, which allows you to become aware of who you are, of your drivers and those of others, and how to respond to challenges in ways that are consistent and emotionally intelligent.

The discussion and definition of what leadership is rages on. In fact, a Google search engine offers 467 million results when 'leadership' is entered into the subject box. However, here are some more popular academic descriptions:

> *Leadership is the behaviour of an individual, directing the activities of a group, towards a shared goal.*
>
> Hemphill and Coons, 1957, p. 7

> *Leadership is exercised when persons mobilize institutional, political, psychological and other resources to arouse, engage and satisfy the motive of followers.*
>
> Burns, 1978, p. 8

> *Leadership is the ability of an individual to influence, motivate and enable others to contribute towards the effectiveness and success of the organisation.*
>
> House *et al.*, 2004, p. 184

Now it might be useful for you to define yourself as a leader. What does it mean to you and what do you achieve as leader in your own context?

EXERCISE 12.1

What kind of leader are you?

▌ How would you define your current leadership style and skills?

▌ What is missing for you and possibly your team?

▌ How would you like to be described as a leader?

▌ What are the steps you need to take to achieve this?

▌ Map your stakeholders – i.e. those who you need to work with to achieve success.

▌ Who are the blockers, facilitators?

One of the big considerations, of course, is that, no matter how powerful you are as an individual leader, you must consider that leadership, not unlike rearing a child, must also be part of the broader social context that includes your followers, organisational systems, the nature of work and cultural environment. This continues to be evidenced in most modern leadership research, which examines leadership at multiple levels of analysis, 'from cognitive through to organisational climates' (Avolio, Walumbwa and Weber, 2009, p. 426). This research continues to help us to understand the contextual variables that mediate the relationship between leaders and followers, which will, in turn, help us to understand the role of environmental complexities and social networks in this relationship (Bono and Anderson, 2005).

How to use EA to become a successful modern leader

Using the seven steps of EA, **outlined in Part 1**, can help you to navigate the role of modern leadership, taking into account the need for you to be powerful as an individual, leader of a team and, indeed, a whole community.

Step 1: The real you

One of the most common questions we are asked as facilitators and consultants is 'What does a good leader look like and how do I become one?' We always reply that there is no one way to lead, but figuring it out starts with knowing yourself. As outlined in Step One, understanding what your values are and how you can live your organisational life close to those around you will allow you to be the most authentic and real leader that you can possibly be. It will not necessarily be perfect but it will be recognised as true and, in turn, will evoke followership.

Step 2: How do you feel and why does it matter?

Your ability to understand how you feel and what emotions are coursing through your body at particular times is crucial to help you make good decisions and avoid getting a reputation as someone who is moody and unpredictable. It will also help you to ensure that you are staying close to your values as your emotional responses will offer you a cue when you are steering off course. This ability will ensure that you do not push yourself to the absolute limits in terms of stress, as, by paying attention to your body, you will understand when your resilience is being eroded.

Step 3: Becoming aware of others

As mentioned in the descriptions and definitions of leadership, you must pay attention to your environment and the context in which you lead. This will allow you to gather very valuable data as to how your team, colleagues and organisation are behaving. It will give you time to spot if their behaviour has changed so that you can carefully find out why and do something to address it before it gets out of control and disrupts productivity. Most leaders fail because they are so busy focused on the microcosms of operations that they fail to see a disengaged workforce and, ultimately, a decline in performance.

Step 4: Understanding the emotions

When people behave strangely or badly, in your view, take some time to figure out what might be really going on. External behaviours often hide the reality of what people are feeling, as most workplaces only appreciate people behaving only rationally and uniformly at work. Therefore, they become experts at heavily disguising what is really going on for them. This also applies to yourself as a leader. When you experience an emotion that seems highly inappropriate to the situation you find yourself in, it is good to stop and reflect about what is going on and what other residual childhood experience may, in fact, be driving the emotion. This will help you to become more emotionally agile in that you can step away from the emotion, study it and make a sensible resolution as to how you might tackle it to ensure that it doesn't keep reoccurring and disrupting your progress.

Step 5: Managing your own emotions

Knowing how you are feeling and why you are feeling this way will give you some useful information as to what reactions are being provoked in you and why. A leader who manages their own emotions is one who is seen as calm and collected, even in the face of the most ambiguous and complex circumstances. The more senior you become as a leader, the more often you will find yourself in a sea of uncertainty with no obvious answer but with just your instinct and experience to guide you to make the best possible decision.

Step 6: Managing the emotions of others

As a leader, this is certainly one of the most challenging aspects of your role, but also one of the most crucial. During our work with leaders, we have found that a lot of organisations hire individuals based on their high IQ, which is perfectly understandable as they want the brightest minds at the helm. However, the shadow of this is that these individuals can often be quite difficult to manage as they are not naturally encouraged to develop their emotional quotient or EQ. Hence, as leader, you can meet some strange behaviours that are difficult to navigate. Your ability to follow the steps above will bring you to a place where reading, understanding and knowing your teams will allow you to manage their emotions when things go wrong. They will trust you to do this, as they will sense that you have their interests at heart. It takes time and practice (and making plenty of mistakes) but it is one of the most powerful skills any successful leader can have.

Step 7: Creating awareness

Take time. Have the confidence to schedule time to think. This is not a luxury or a nice-to-have, this is an absolute necessity for you to be effective as a leader. It will still your mind and help you notice what is happening both inside and outside yourself so that you can understand and manage such behaviours. This will ensure that the people who meet you meet a calm, measured and poised leader who is ready for anything. It will also pull your mind from the weeds so that you can think about the future and how your team and organisation can optimise their skills and activities to be the very best that they can be. Developing a routine of mindfulness or simply taking the time to think will increase your own resilience and ensure that you expend less energy on a day-to-day basis. This can only be good for your health and tenure as a leader.

Building your leadership brand

Once you have taken and used the seven steps of EA to enhance your leadership abilities, you can now create your own unique leadership brand to increase your impact and influence. When we mention global brands such as Apple, Coca-Cola and BMW, they all conjure up certain images in our minds and often evoke our sensory abilities. One could say that this is simply the power of marketing and media. However, the analogy of brand can also apply to you and your leadership in your own organisation and among your team. The reason for this is that people make judgements, sometimes unfairly, based on how you behave or how they experience you at work. They may have heard a story about you from another colleague with whom you disagreed and unintentionally, but consequently, upset. Someone may speak badly of you and this image remains in the minds of the people who hear it until they experience you first-hand. Even then, you may struggle to overcome such unfair prejudice, but this is, unfortunately, the nature of human behaviour.

> ## As a successful leader it is important to take control of your leadership brand

Therefore, as a successful leader it is important to take control of your leadership brand. This means that you can cleverly cultivate an image that you can realistically live up to, so that your people can start to see a consistent version of you as a leader. You can do this by asking yourself the following questions and by subsequently following the steps outlined.

EXERCISE 12.2

Creating your leadership brand

You have just been assigned to another division of the organisation. You are due to meet your team on Monday morning and you have been asked to address them as a group. You don't know them, but they have heard of you. You have some time to prepare and consider some of the following questions:

▌ What do you want your leadership brand to represent? How will you achieve this?

▌ What is your vision for the organisation/division/team?

▌ What will be your opening remarks?

▌ How will you both communicate your own values and tap into those of the new team?

▌ How will you engage them?

▌ What are the three key takeaways that they will remember about you and your leadership brand?

Prior to this address, prepare your speech and record it either visually or via an audio device. When you play it back, listen and watch carefully for the non-verbal messages that you are conveying. Instigate the help of a trusted colleague to assess your performance and offer feedback. It is useful to practise your speech and redo it as necessary. Even if you are not meeting a new team, it is also a good way to sit down and really assess how you want your leadership image to be conveyed. Try to use all of the emotional agility skills that we have outlined above.

Your ability to influence as a leader

Once you have cultivated a consistent and an authentic leadership brand you will have some chance of influencing those you meet. The highly successful sister publication to this book, *The Leader's Guide to Influencing* (Dent and Brent, 2010), offers some keen insights into how you can achieve success as a leader. You will notice that the skills of influencing are highly related to the skills of emotional agility. Some of these skills include:

- **Listening and probing.** Ask open questions and actively listen to the response. Use the Coaching Feedback model (mentioned in Chapter 8) to help you design some questions that you can easily ask.

- **Verbal fluency.** Find a way to articulate your points in a thoughtful but powerful way that has impact and meaning.

- **Rapport building.** Take the time to build relationships with your stakeholders. Even if you don't have an immediate reason to connect with the person, make the time to get to know people and understand their values. It will also help to quietly promote your leadership brand.

- **Awareness of non-verbal communication.** When you have developed a skill set to pick up your own emotions, you will be much more in control of how you behave, as you will be far more poised and measured. You will also begin to pay more attention to how others around you are behaving non-verbally, which will allow you to gather useful data on how a conversation or interaction is progressing in order to achieve the desired outcome.

▌**Preparation.** As discussed throughout this book, taking the time to prepare, whether it is assessing, understanding and managing your emotions and behaviours prior to any planned interaction, will allow you to make much more informed decisions that are not driven by runaway emotions. When undertaking management activities, such as performance reviews or engaging a team, you must spend time thinking through your preferred outcome.

▌**Trust.** In order for people to follow you, they must believe you are legitimate and will protect their interests. Trust is achieved when people see evidence that you are someone who has interests that are beyond your own self-fulfilment and actively help, encourage and support others in their quest for happiness and success. Living by a clear set of values and endeavouring not to waver on these in times of crisis is something that others see as admirable, and can achieve great influence.

▌**Courage.** Having the courage to stand up for what is right is often a huge attraction for followers in your team. It is seen as powerful when a leader goes out to battle for their team and protects them at all costs. This warrior-like characteristic often instils great loyalty in followers. It is often a strong emotional response that will help you find this courage.

▌**Self-knowledge.** Those leaders who know themselves intimately, flaws and all, are often seen to have shed their egos and possess true humility. Narcissistic and egotistical leaders are fun to follow initially but teams often discover that most of these leaders' activities are to promote their own interests, such as progressing their careers and ambitions.

▌**Enthusiasm.** Creating a mood that encourages people to flock to you is a key element of how good your influencing abilities are. When you are working in a context where your values are satisfied, you will notice that you are much happier and, consequently, you will spread that mood in your wake. Most leaders who are optimistic and visionary are passionately followed by their teams, peers and stakeholders. No matter how bad your day has been, try listing at least two positive things that have happened to you that day.

Hang in there

As you can see, being a leader is a mammoth task that can often be overwhelming, exhausting and feel like a thankless occupation. You often have only solved only one problem when another presents itself and you need to step in to resolve another. The work frequently requires great discretion, as you are dealing with people and their sensitivities, which often need to be kept confidential. Therefore, it can be hard to offer evidence to others of what you have achieved in your everyday role as a leader. However, most good leaders are ones who keep the ship steady, their people happy and motivated and step in calmly and with poise when things start to go wrong. This chapter demonstrates that you are not just in charge of your team but also need to work hard to consider the context you are operating in. Your skills in emotional agility will help you to do this well and also increase and maintain your influence.

IN SUMMARY

This chapter offers some suggestions as to what leadership is and how you can use the steps outlined to evolve your leadership brand and increase your impact as a consequence. It offers some strategies that you can use to increase your influencing abilities, and shows how these, combined with your emotional agility, will offer you a powerful means to induce followership.

Conclusion

This book offers some keen insights on how to become an emotionally agile leader. It gives you the opportunity to take the time to understand yourself and your values, what you stand for and why and how it affects your everyday interactions with the world around you. In order to help you figure this out, the book lists seven steps to help you build your skills in emotional agility, which allows you to reflect on the type of leader you currently are and what type of leader you would like to be. As you have probably gathered, leadership is not an easy skill to learn and leading academics have been puzzled about how to achieve it. The fact that you have chosen to read this book suggests that you are interested in developing yourself and those around you through taking the time to reflect and discover what is important to you, how you behave and why.

The world looks forward to meeting you as a great leader

Our work with leaders has led us to conclude that the most powerful leaders are those who have taken the time to do this, perhaps forcibly because something life-changing or earth-shattering has happened to them. Or perhaps they found themselves at a crossroads in their lives or careers where they needed to stop and think about what to do next. These people emerge as leaders who have the courage, wisdom and patience to see that the key to success is the time they take to prioritise their relationships with those around them and that the success of performance outcomes seamlessly follows. Enjoy your journey and reflection. The world looks forward to meeting you as a great leader who can make a difference and have a lasting and important legacy.

What did you think of this book?

We're really keen to hear from you about this book, so that we can make our publishing even better.

Please log on to the following website and leave us your feedback.

It will only take a few minutes and your thoughts are invaluable to us.

www.pearsoned.co.uk/bookfeedback

Appendices

A pplication of emotional agility to your own leader-ship journey is one that will allow you to navigate many contexts in the workplace. However, it is also useful to see its current application across mainstream business, from its role in the hiring of chief executives, to understanding how negative emotions can affect work rela-tionships, to enhancing negotiation strategies. The following three articles offer some keen insight into the extensive appli-cation and role of emotional agility in contemporary business and demonstrate both its usefulness and hindrance, if man-aged badly.

Article 1

Almost twenty-five years ago, Daniel Goleman suggested that IQ was not enough to succeed as a manager and suggested that an alternative intelligence called emotional intelligence (EQ) was required to navigate the tricky path of management. This article suggests that such sentiments are still as relevant today as they ever were, as Bill Gates can testify.

To pick a know-all chief executive is just plain dumb

By Andrew Hill

Financial Times June 29, 2015

When Deutsche Bank named John Cryan as its new chief executive three weeks ago, the commentary had an insidious subtext. He has 'an enormous brain', one friend told the *FT*. 'Very thoughtful', said a former colleague. Ominously for Mr Cryan, these comments echoed those made about Vikram Pandit when he unexpectedly stepped down as Citigroup's CEO in 2012. He was 'too cerebral', said critics of the Citi boss.

The implication in both cases is that being a brainbox is a disqualification for running some of the largest and most technically complex companies. I was brought up to respect and pursue academic success, but while it grates that the world believes analytically minded swots rarely make great business leaders, the world is right (even if Mr Cryan ultimately turns out to be one of the few exceptions).

No less an intellect than Bill Gates told an invited *FT* audience last week that his background (learning about the world by reading an encyclopaedia, starting at A for Aardvark) made him think at first that the obvious corporate hierarchy would be one based on IQ, with the brightest at the top.

It took only a few years running a business for Mr Gates to realise he had made a colossal error, one that would have doomed Microsoft had he pursued it. 'By the age of 25, I knew that IQ comes in different forms', he said. '[Understanding] sales and management seems to be negatively correlated with writing good code or understanding physics equations. That was befuddling for me.'

Mr Gates was brought up in an age when IQ testing was popular, before it was revealed that the tests themselves could disadvantage some groups and that such tests measured attributes that were irrelevant in some workplaces. Would you, for instance, rather be rescued by an out of condition firefighter with Mensa membership or a fit one of average IQ with a decade of experience in extinguishing infernos?

The *FT* asks successful people in its weekly Inventory feature if they have ever undergone an IQ test. Many have. But none that I can recall has said the result had any bearing on their later success. There is a reason why the description of Enron's senior executives as 'the smartest guys in the room' was a harbinger of dysfunction and disaster and not a qualification for flexible leadership.

Yet even though the idea that chief executives are omnipotent is fading, the myth of the omniscient corporate boss persists. Leaders remain reluctant to admit publicly that they simply cannot know everything about their business, until an operational blunder or a scandal reveals the truth.

One reason CEOs try to appear all-knowing is that their public appearances – the analyst briefing, the television interview, the conference panel – place unrealistic pressure on imperfect individuals to demonstrate perfect knowledge. At such events, executives are preoccupied with not appearing thick. It would be far more realistic and refreshing if they admitted that, day to day, they often call on lieutenants to answer tricky questions.

The best chief executives do not spend hours alone, applying their 'enormous brains' to business problems. When academics from Warwick and Oxford Saïd business schools followed leaders in the healthcare sector for a study published in the latest *MIT Sloan Management Review*, they found that each built a 'personal knowledge infrastructure', which consisted of many elements. This infrastructure includes time for thought – one health manager had what he called a 'train pile' of research that he could read while travelling. But it also allows for visits to the wards in off-hours to spot problems, analysis of a data 'dashboard' of corporate performance and consultations with an inner circle of colleagues.

I see two intelligent ways that clever leaders can apply their IQs: as entrepreneurial founders and as part of a balanced team. Mr Gates did not propose snuffing out bright sparks in business, or switching them for executives with the more modish 'EQ' of emotional intelligence. He talked instead about the importance of fishing from three different 'IQ pools'.

To meet his current philanthropic goals, he says, he tries to mix managers with 'scientific understanding, business analytics and a passion for being out in the field'. The same should go for all organisations: leading them in any other way would be plain stupid.

Article 2

The experience of strong emotions can sometimes be overwhelming and cause people to act in a way that is viewed by others as irrational or out of character. As you have read throughout the book, people are sometimes driven by their Child ego state, which triggers reactions in an adult context. This article helpfully examines how some of these negative emotions can, if assessed and understood, be adapted to pursue a more positive outcome. It involves some reflection on and understanding of the cause of the feeling and on how to manage it in order to ensure a more productive result for all those involved. Emotional agility at its best.

Surviving the success of others

By Naomi Shragai

Financial Times April 16, 2014

It is one of the most shameful feelings to admit – the twinge of joy experienced when a colleague fails. Although you would prefer to be the person who celebrates your colleague's success, you are not, you are envious. The guilt for having such ungenerous and negative thoughts leaves you feeling even worse.

Envy, one of the most excruciating feelings, is not just desiring what your colleague has achieved, it is wanting to destroy what he has because his success has come to feel like your misfortune. Rather than trying to understand how he achieved his position and how you could improve in this regard by healthy competition, you are convinced that the unfairness of the situation justifies a retaliation.

This can explain why good ideas are trashed at meetings, why malicious gossip is spread and why extremely competitive work environments underperform or even fail. Indeed, while envy is usually thought of as an individual problem, when hidden and not managed it can damage a company's operational and financial performance.

Individually, it damages the person himself, as one film producer discovered. He explains how his feelings of envy eventually spoilt his capacity to take pleasure in his own success.

'It is a horrible feeling when you see someone release a film and you are willing it to do badly, it can make you feel very disgusted about yourself. You feel deep down that it is wrong – it doesn't really enhance your success', he says.

'Initially it can give you an adrenalin rush but then it can make you feel very low and induces a sense of self-loathing. What starts out as aggressive feelings outward, turns inwards on yourself. You are feeling rotten because of what you have become, so that even when you are successful you can undermine that sense of pleasure because somehow [envy] spoils the process.'

He also believes the issue has reached epidemic proportions through social media. 'When in the past I may have got a bad review, I got pleasure in the fact that someone may not have read it. Now, you can be damned sure that the bloody thing has been pinged to thousands of people you know.'

Envy often originates from early sibling relationships. For a woman who worked in retailing and was consumed by envious feelings towards a younger and attractive woman in the office, the situation replicated her relationship with her younger brother, whom she hated for gaining their parents' adoration, leaving her feeling ignored.

The woman adds: 'She had usurped my position, I think she had the ear of the manager, he loved the fact that she was hungry and driven. She knew how to get attention because she had the vitality I didn't have.'

Because of the shame and sinister connotations associated with envy, it is rarely discussed or acknowledged and is difficult to identify. Secrecy makes it worse – when envy is hidden or denied it is most dangerous. The underlying rage and hatred are often pushed into the unconscious while the envious feelings are acted out indirectly through destructive behaviours.

An example is a woman in publishing whose career had reached a plateau, and who then spent every hiring meeting undercutting the competence of potentially threatening candidates while supporting the lesser qualified and hence non-threatening ones. Her negative comments contaminated the decision process and prevented more competent people from being employed by the company.

It is difficult to rid oneself of envious feelings, and indeed they are found at all levels of organisations. Not only does it exist among peer colleagues, and from staff towards their managers, executives can also envy subordinates, and even people they mentor, as one manager revealed to me: 'You hire clever people but you don't want them to be too clever in case they outshine you. The truth is I liked it when they were doing well, but not too well.' Mark Stein, professor of leadership and management at Leicester University in the UK, says business leaders' fear of being usurped by subordinates with outstanding skills and leadership ability makes envy 'the real issue in leadership succession'.

'If you know you are going to retire, it's difficult to find space in your heart to help someone take on your position and do it well', he says. 'The real fear is that they can do it better.' He says that although a moderate amount of envy is necessary for acquiring leadership positions, for bosses to acknowledge their envy would imply recognising the limits of their own achievements.

Research by Tanya Menon, associate professor of management at Ohio State University, reveals how envy interferes with knowledge-sharing and innovation because envious people are more likely to dismiss and undervalue their colleagues' ideas than learn from them. 'From my work I noticed that people tend to learn much more readily from external competitors than internal competitors. Most research says that people favour their in-group members, people who share a common identity. But in business we see exactly the opposite. Someone in your own organisation is much more threatening because they directly compete with you for bonuses and promotions. Someone outside the firm doesn't directly compete for the rewards.'

Prof Menon studied a merger where the decision to buy another company for its knowledge and people had backfired. 'When the firms were competitors, there was significant learning', she explains. 'However, after the acquisition happened, the outsider became the insider and they started derogating the very things that they had been admiring initially.

'This is the interesting thing about envy – it's precisely because something or someone reveals excellence that people do not want to learn from it.'

How resentment at work can be constructive

With awareness and emotional intelligence – alongside a willingness to tolerate uncomfortable feelings – conscious envy can be transformed for the good. If you can recognise that what you are experiencing is envy and not unfairness, you can then be challenged to seek out what you find desirable in the other person and change envy to constructive thinking.

Quy Huy, associate professor of strategy at Insead, believes a balance of negative emotions, such as envy and discontent, alongside positive emotions, such as pride and hope, is what drives people to improve themselves. 'It's the yin and yang, it's like having a good opposition political party, it keeps people on their toes.'

He says employers need 'organisational emotional intelligence', deploying warm emotion, not cold rationality, to channel envy into healthy competition. 'The difference between competition and envy is in how you regulate your emotions – [the former] is to improve yourself, and the other is to destroy the other person.'

He argues that companies should scrap stacked ranking evaluation systems, in which employee performance for reward and firing purposes is forced into fixed categories such as the top 10 per cent or bottom 30 per cent. These tend to create unhealthy competitive structures that fuel envy and lead to overall company underperformance because people are less likely to share knowledge and help each other.

Companies should instead invest in what he describes as 'collective emotional capital'. 'This involves creating a safe place for people to express their negative emotions. This takes away the stigma and secrecy associated with envy, and so helps to eliminate destructive consequences. You have to remind and reassure people that they are valued. You also have to give them hope that if they start something today, they will also be rewarded sometime in the future.'

The writer is a psychotherapist and this article is based partly on her clinical experience.

 Source: Shragai, N. (2014) Surviving the success of others, *Financial Times*, 16 April 2014.
© The Financial Times Ltd 2014. All Rights Reserved.

Article 3

Throughout this book, it has been demonstrated how emotional agility can be used in leadership contexts to manage performance, increase the performance of teams, increase creativity and innovation and manage change. This article further demonstrates how emotions can assist during negotiations by equipping you with awareness skills of both yourself and others and how you can optimally observe and manage any emotions to ensure a positive outcome. It offers some insight into the role of visualisation and how this can improve the possibility of success as you will subconsciously work towards achieving your goal.

Emotions as a negotiating tool

By Alicia Clegg

Financial Times February 5, 2014

Nelson Mandela famously spent some of his time in prison studying Afrikaner history and teaching himself Afrikaans, the language of his jailers. He understood that being able to see the world through the eyes of his adversaries would be important in any future negotiations.

Empathy and emotions – both one's own and those of the other side – play a crucial role in negotiating and dealmaking, whether in politics or in business. Emotional awareness can help you navigate blind spots and prejudices and arm you with self-control. In the recently published book, *The Art of Negotiation: How to Improvise Agreement in a Chaotic World,* Professor Michael Wheeler of Harvard Business School likens the skill of good negotiators to that of jazz musicians or comedians who improvise. Artists such as these know how to read each other's moods, respond creatively to unexpected twists and turns and run with a theme.

If you break sweat at the mere thought of negotiating, Prof Wheeler says, the danger is that you will handcuff yourself with rigid plans, miss opportunities to solve problems creatively or settle too low. But, even if you are as cool as a cucumber, you still need to understand that others may not be. 'As people we like to be in control; as negotiators we need others to say yes', explains Prof Wheeler. It is possible to ready yourself emotionally as part of the mental preparation for negotiating. Counterintuitively, resolving not to be nervous may do more harm than good since it diverts your attention from the other party to yourself. A better approach, says Prof Wheeler, is to turn anxiety into curiosity by listening intently to what the other side says and how they say it. Words, body language and subtle variations in vocal tone all give clues to the other party's preoccupations, helping the emotionally perceptive negotiator to spot opportunities for agreement that others miss.

As Prof Wheeler points out in his book: 'If you are deeply attentive, your mind will be quieted'. Insights from neuroscience and psychology suggest ways for negotiators to achieve emotional balance and prime themselves to succeed. For instance, recalling past achievements encourages optimism. Experiments that measure hormone release have shown that walking tall reduces anxiety. Erin Egan, a senior manager in business development at Microsoft in the US, tries to channel her nerves into excitement, rather than suppress them. 'I try to visualise an outcome that will be really positive and tell myself we're going to get to a really great place.'

Although this sounds simplistic, it may have scientific justification. In experiments by Harvard researchers, volunteers told to say 'I'm excited' while performing stressful tasks outshone those instructed to say 'I'm calm'. The idea is that it is easier to shift from anxiety to excitement than from anxiety to calm. When it comes to working on the psyche of the opposite camp, businesspeople might learn from what works – and does not work – for diplomats and peacekeepers negotiating in hotspots where the stakes can be life or death. Jeff Weiss, an adjunct professor at West Point, the US military academy, and partner at management consultant Vantage Partners, argues that the same principles apply whether in combat zones or conference rooms. He draws a parallel between an incident from the US engagement in Afghanistan and commercial disputes that he encounters in consultancy. In the Afghan example, western intelligence officers wrongly detained a village leader for a year. They had assumed from calls to his mobile that he was an insurgent. In fact, the local Taliban was threatening him for opening a girls' school.

The man demanded an apology and improved procedures, not simply compensation. However, the approach of the officer handling his settlement was to increase the proposed payout, without addressing his concerns or attempting to salve his hurt. The village leader ended up wealthier but more embittered, and vowed never again to trust westerners and advised his neighbours not to either. The officer had made a classic negotiation mistake that businesses that feel themselves to be on shaky ground often make too: trying to take a short-cut to a settlement by buying goodwill rather than engaging in the painstaking business of repairing trust. As Mr Weiss says: 'If you don't show empathy, if you don't dig into a problem to figure out the cause and make sure it won't happen again, you won't fix a relationship, no matter how much compensation you pay.' Of course, you may listen, probe and empathise and still not achieve a meeting of minds. Some negotiations, by their nature, are essentially just haggles over price. Sometimes one side may see opportunities to expand the size of the pie by negotiating creatively, but the other just wants to drive the hardest bargain it can.

To stay on the front foot, says Prof Wheeler, consummate negotiators – like improv artists – need a repertoire of responses to call upon. 'If someone is being utterly unreasonable and misstating facts, and you've tried correcting them politely and got nowhere, you might hammer the table to get their attention,' he says. But such displays should be undertaken strategically to serve a well thought-out purpose – 'not because you have flown off the handle'. Even with careful emotional preparation, however, talks can sometimes fail because, in the heat of the moment, negotiators mishear or misread each other's motives, detecting slights where none were meant. Experienced negotiators have a number of gambits for cooling things down when emotions run high. One of the simplest and most effective is to take a break. Another, popularised by the conflict mediator William Ury, author of *Getting Past No*, is to picture yourself on a balcony observing the negotiation from outside. When you step back in, your opposite number may still be unyielding, but your perception of the situation may have changed.

Michael McIlwrath, head of litigation for General Electric's oil and gas division, offers a personal example. He once spent three frustrating months trying to hammer out a settlement with a combative advocate from a large European energy group. With relations on a knife edge, his opponent suggested a solution so unorthodox and financially complex that he dismissed it as mischief-making. It was only when a colleague to whom he unburdened himself responded, 'oh, interesting . . . sounds like a pretty good idea', that he realised the suggestion was ingenious and good for both sides. 'We went from a bad dispute to [a settlement that] both companies regarded as a huge win and it led to a business relationship that [endures] to this day.' As a demonstration of the adage 'we see things not as they are, but as we are', you could not want for a better example, he believes.

The jazz player's guide to improvising a deal

In negotiation as in jazz, it is impossible to anticipate every twist and turn, says Michael Wheeler of Harvard Business School. Skilful improvisers:

- Pay heed: By paying close attention to what others express through body language, words and tone of voice, improvisers spot opportunities for agreement that others miss.

- Complement and go solo. Like virtuoso musicians, top negotiators know when to lead and when to give others the stage.

- Change tempo. This is as important as knowing how to harmonise. If talks are deadlocked, posing a surprising question may sometimes unlock them. If an opponent is unreasonable you may need to bang the table, say 'no' loudly or walk away – but it should be you, not your emotions that make the choice.

- Stockpile fall-backs and get-outs for when inspiration fails. If you are stuck on one point, try moving to another. If tempers fray, take a break.

- Fit plans to reality, not reality to plans. Game-plans should be treated as hypotheses to test, reshape or discard – not as scripts.

Source: Clegg, A. (2014) Emotions as a negotiating tool, *Financial Times*, 5 February 2014.

References

Acs, Z.J. and Audretsch, D.B. (1988) 'Innovation in large and small firms: an empirical analysis about what they do', *American Economic Review*, 78: 678–690.

Adkins, A. (2015) 'Majority of U.S. Employees Not Engaged Despite Gains in 2014', **www.gallup.com**. Accessed 18 May 2015.

Agnew, H. (2014) 'Mindfulness gives stressed out bankers something to think about', *Financial Times*, 4 May.

Amabile, T.M. (1988) 'A model of creativity and innovation in organisations', *Research in Organisational Behaviour*, 10: 123–67.

Avolio, B.J., Walumbwa, F.O., Weber, T.J. (2009) 'Leadership: current theories, research and future directions', *Annual Review of Psychology*, 60: 421–49.

Babiak, P. and Hare, R.D. (2007) *Snakes in Suits: When Psychopaths Go To Work*, HarperCollins: New York.

Barnes, S., Brown, K.W., Krusemark, E., Campbell, W.K., Rogge, R.D. (2007) 'The role of mindfulness in romantic relationship satisfaction and responses to relationship stress', *Journal of Marital and Family Therapy*, 33: 482–500.

Berne, E. (1964). *Games People Play – The Basic Hand* Book *of Transactional Analysis*, Ballantine Books: New York.

Bono, E. and Anderson, M. (2005) 'The advice and influence networks of transformational leaders', *Journal of Applied Psychology*, 90(6).

Bridges, W. (2009) *Managing Transitions: Making the Most of Change*, Nicholas Brealey Publishing: London. 3rd edition.

Burns, J.M. (1978) *Leadership*, Harper and Row: New York.

Cahn, B.R. and Polich, J. (2006) 'Meditation states and traits: eeg, erp, and neuroimaging studies', *Psychological Bulletin*, 132: 180–211.

Cain, S. (2012) *Quiet: The Power of Introverts in a World That Can't Stop Talking*, Crown Publishing: New York.

Cainelli, G., Evangelista, R., Savona, M. (2006) 'Innovation and economic performance in service firms', *Cambridge Journal of Economics*, 30(3): 435–58.

Camelo-Ordaz, C., Hernandez-Lara, A.B., Valle-Cabrera, R. (2005) 'The relationship between top management teams and innovative capacity in companies', *Journal of Management Development*, 24(8): 683–705.

Carmody, J. and Baer, R.A. (2008) 'Relationships between mindfulness practice and levels of mindfulness, medical and psychological symptoms and well-being in a mindfulness-based stress reduction program', *Journal of Behavioral Medicine*, 31: 23–33.

Caruso, K. (2012) 'Development at the top. Use the 9 box grid to develop talent in succession planning, www.webvia.people.com Accessed 12 April 2015.

Chambers, R., Lo, B.C.Y., Allen, N.B. (2008) 'The impact of intensive mindfulness training on attentional control, cognitive style, and affect', *Cognitive Therapy and Research*, 32: 303–22.

Clark, J. (2015) 'A guide to surviving the office psychopath'. http://www.yourlifeworks.ninemsn.com/article.aspx?id=373544 Accessed 22 April 2015.

Coffey, K. A. and Hartman, M. (2008) 'Mechanisms of action in the inverse relationship between mindfulness and psychological distress', *Complementary Health Practice Review*, 13: 79–91.

Coombs, R. and Miles, I. (2000) 'Innovation, measurement and services, the new problematique', in S.J. Metcalfe and I. Miles (eds), *Innovation Systems in the Service Sectors: Measurement and Case Study Analysis*, Kluwer: Boston, Dordrecht and London, 85–104.

David, S. and Congleton, C. (2013) 'Emotional agility', *Harvard Business Review*, November.

Davidson, R.J., Kabat-Zinn, J., Schumacher, J., Rosenkranz, M., Muller, D., Santorelli, S.F. and Sheridan, J.F. (2003) 'Alterations in brain and immune function produced by mindfulness meditation', *Psychosomatic Medicine*, 66: 149–52.

Davis, D.M. and Hayes, J.A. (2012) 'What are the benefits of mindfulness?', *American Psychological Association Journal*, 43(7) (July/August).

Day, A. and Lubitsh, G. (2012) 'Mutual trust is essential for successful change: lessons from implementing NHS reforms', *360° The Ashridge Journal*, Autumn: 13–21.

Dekeyser, M., Raes, F., Leijssen, M., Leyson, S. and Dewulf, D. (2008) 'Mindfulness skills and interpersonal behavior', *Personality and Individual Differences*, 44: 1235–45.

Dent, F.E. and Brent, M. (2010) *The Leader's Guide to Influence: How to Use Soft Skills to Get Hard Results*, Pearson: London.

Fisher, C.D. (1997) *Moods and Emotions While Working – Missing Pieces of Job Satisfaction*, Bond University [Queensland] School of Business Discussion Papers (No. 64).

Fleming, K. (2012) 'Strategic leadership of architectural firms, the role of emotion management and innovation', Doctoral Dissertation, Dublin City University, Ireland (Unpublished).

Grossman, P., Niemann, L., Schmidt, S. and Walach, H. (2004) 'Mindfulness-based stress reduction and health benefits: a meta-analysis', *Journal of Psychosomatic Research*, 57: 35–43.

Hare, R. and Babiak, P. (2006) *Snakes in Suits: When Psychopaths Go to Work*, Harper Business: New York.

Harris, T. (2004) *I'm OK, You're OK*, Harper Collins: New York.

Hatfield, E., Cacioppo, J.T. and Rapson, R.L. (1994) *Emotional Contagion*, Cambridge University Press: New York.

http://www.helpguide.org

http://www.healthysleep.med.harvard.edu

Helliwell, J.F., Layard, R. and Sachs, J. (2015) *The World Happiness Report,* United Nations.

Hemphill, J.K. and Coons, A.E. (1957) 'Development of the leader behaviour description questionnaire', in R.M. Stodgill and A.E. Coons (eds), *Leader Behaviour: Its Description and Measurement*, Columbus: Bureau of Business Research, Ohio State University.

Hoffman, S.G., Sawyer, A.T., Witt, A.A. and Oh, D. (2010) 'The effect of mindfulness-based therapy on anxiety and depression: a meta-analytic review', *Journal of Consulting and Clinical Psychology*, 78: 169–83.

House, R.J., Hanges, P.J., Javidan, M., Doffman, P.W., Gupta, V. and Associates (2004) *Leadership, Culture and Organisations: The Globe Study of 62 Societies*, Sage: Thousand Oaks, CA.

Izard, C.E. (2009) 'Emotion theory and research: highlights, unanswered questions, and emerging issues', *Annual Review of Psychology*, Issue 1: 1–25.

Jha, A.P., Stanley, E.A., Kiyonaga, A., Wong, L. and Gelfand, L. (2010) 'Examining the protective effects of mindfulness training on working memory capacity and affective experience', *Emotion*, 10: 54–64.

Kotter, J.P. (1996) *Leading Change*, Harvard Business School Press.

Kotter, J.P. (2001) 'What leaders really do', *Harvard Business Review*, December.

Kübler-Ross, E. (1969) *On Death and Dying*, Scribner: New York.

Levitt, T. (1969) 'Exploit the business life cycle', *Harvard Business Review*, November.

Luft, J. and Ingham, H. (1955). 'The Johari Window, a graphic model of interpersonal awareness', *Proceedings of the Western Training Laboratory in Group Development* (University of California, Los Angeles).

Luthans, F. and Avolio, B.J. (2003) 'Authentic leadership: a positive developmental approach', in K.S. Cameron, J.E. Dutton and R.E. Quinn (eds), *Positive Organisational Scholarship: Foundations of a New Discipline*. Berrett Koehler: San Francisco, 241–58.

Lutz, A., Slagter, H.A., Rawlings, N.B., Francis, A.D., Greischar, L.L. and Davidson, R.J. (2009) 'Mental training enhances attentional stability: neural and behavioral evidence', *The Journal of Neuroscience*, 29: 13418–27.

Mayer, J. and Salovey, P. (2002) *The Mayer Salovey and Caruso Emotional Intelligence Test, Version 2.0*, Multi Health Systems: Toronto, Ontario, Canada.

Moore, A. and Malinowski, P. (2009) 'Meditation, mindfulness and cognitive flexibility', *Consciousness and Cognition*, 18: 176–86.

NESTA (2009) 'Measuring sectoral innovation capability in nine areas of the UK economy', Report for NESTA Innovation index project by S. Roper, C. Hales, J.R. Bryson and J. Love.

Ortner, C.N.M., Kilner, S.J. and Zelazo, P.D. (2007) 'Mindfulness, meditation and reduced emotional interference on a cognitive task', *Motivation and Emotion*, 31: 271–83.

Ostafin, B.D., Chawla, N., Bowen, S., Dillworth, T.M., Witkiewitz, K. and Marlatt, G.A. (2006) 'Intensive mindfulness training and the reduction of psychological distress: a preliminary study', *Cognitive and Behavioral Practice*, 13: 191–7.

Plutchik, R. (1994) *The Psychology and Biology of Emotion*, New York: Harper Collins.

Shaver, P.R., Schwartz, J.C. and Wu, S. (1992) 'Cross cultural similarities and differences in emotion and its representation: a prototype approach', *Review of Personality and Social Psychology*, 13, ed. M.S. Clark, Sage: Beverly Hills, CA, 175–212.

Russell, J.A. (1980) 'A circumplex model of affect', *Journal of Personality and Social Psychology*, 39: 1161–78. (An alternative circular model but with different labelled dimensions was proposed by D. Watson and A. Tellegen, 'Towards a consensual structure of mood', *Psychological Bulletin*, 98 (1985), 219–35.)

Shipton, H., West, M.A., Dawson, J., Birdi, K. and Patterson, M. (2006) 'HRM as predictor of innovation', *Human Resource Management Journal*, 16(1).

Siegel, D.J. (2007) 'Mindfulness training and neural integration: differentiation of distinct streams of awareness and the cultivation of well-being', *Social Cognitive and Affective Neuroscience*, 2: 259–63.

Strength Deployment Inventory (SDI), self-assessment tool. Publisher: Personal Strengths UK Ltd.

Tether, B.S. (2005) 'So services innovate (differently)? Insights from the European innobarometer survey', *Industry and Innovation*, 12(2): 153–84.

Van Velsor, E. and Brittain, J.L. (1995) 'Why executives derail: perspectives across time and cultures', *The Academy of Management Executive*, 9(4) (November), 62–72 .

Wachs, K. and Cordova, J.V. (2007) 'Mindful relating: exploring mindfulness and emotion repertoires in intimate relationships', *Journal of Marital and Family Therapy*, 33: 464–81.

Waller, L. and Reitz, M. (2015) 'The neuroscience of management development', in P. Hind (ed.), *Management Development that Works*, Libri Publishing: Faringdon.

West, M.A. (2002) 'Sparkling fountains or stagnant ponds: an integrative model of creativity and innovation implementation in work groups', *Applied Psychology: An International Review*, 51: 355–424.

Wilson, C. (2010) The Coaching Feedback model, **http://www.coachingcultureatwork.com** Accessed 25 May 2015.

Yuvaraj, S. and Srivastava, N. (2007) 'Are innovative managers emotionally intelligent?' *Journal of Management Research*, 7(3): 169–78.

Index